BOOK ONE:
MAKING QUILTS FROM VINTAGE BLOCKS

TREASURES
from Yesteryear

SHARON NEWMAN

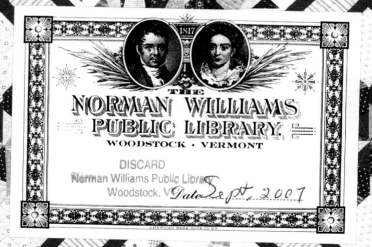

That
Patchwork
Place®

Credits

Editor-in-Chief . . . . Barbara Weiland
Technical Editor . . . . Janet White
Managing Editor . . . . Greg Sharp
Copy Editor . . . . Tina Cook
Proofreader . . . . Leslie Phillips
Design Director . . . . Judy Petry
Text and Cover Designer . . . . Cheryl Senecal
Design Assistant . . . . Claudia L'Heureux
Photographer . . . . Brent Kane
Illustrator . . . . Laurel Strand
Illustration Assistant . . . . Lisa McKenney

Treasures from Yesteryear: Book One
© 1995 by Sharon Newman
That Patchwork Place, Inc., PO Box 118, Bothell,
WA 98041-0118 USA

Printed in Hong Kong
00 99 98 97 96 95   6 5 4 3 2 1

Library of Congress Cataloging-in-Publication Data

Newman, Sharon
        Treasures from yesteryear / Sharon Newman.
            p.   cm.
        ISBN 1–56477–039–7 (v. 1 : pbk.)
        1. Quilting—Patterns.   2. Patchwork—Patterns.
    3. Strip quilting—Patterns.   I. Title.
    TT835.N476 1995
    746.46—dc20   94-38618
                                                    CIP

MISSION STATEMENT

Acknowledgments

Many thanks to the quilt owners who gra-
ciously loaned their quilts to be photographed:
Joyce Braus, Flora and H. R. Bryan, Sue Caraway, Kay Jackson Fleming, Jackie French,
Frances Hambright, Betty Mills, Bessie Sawyer Newman, Mary Phy, Jackie Rayroux, Margaret Reid, and Harold and Charlotte Simms.

Special appreciation for reproduction and
vintage fabrics is expressed to fellow fabric fa-
natics: Cacilie Daily, Dianne Ferguson,
Dorothymae Groves, Emily Hooper, Nancy
Kirk, Jackie Reis, Cindy Rennels, Eileen
Trestain, Peggy Vannoy, Louise Wood, and
Julia Zgliniec.

Exceptional quilting services were provided
by Claudia Brownfield (1898 Stars in Garden
Maze), Ethel Burkleo (Double Wedding Ring
and Lone Star), Florence Kirby (Embroidered
Collage), Geraldine Powell (Crow's Nest), and
Lorene Weir (Stars and Ninepatches).

The quilts would not have been completed
without miles of binding made by Doris
Hagens; hours of marking by Etta McFarland;
precision cutting by Julia Templer, Tracy
Faulkner, and Sonja Bray; and continuous encouragement from Roxi Eppler, Carrie Lou
Holtman, Denise Kyle, Sue McGann, Carol
Newman, and Barbara Phiffer. Jackie Reis of
Accu-Pattern Drafting Service provided special
assistance in every area: drafting patterns,
making templates, computing yardage, sug-
gesting settings, planning quilting designs, and
reminding me to eat! Vicki Newman Potts gen-
erously gave editorial assistance and hours of
proofreading.

My most heartfelt respect and appreciation
goes to the anonymous ladies who chose the
patterns, arranged the fabrics, and stitched the
blocks and pieces that now, after all the years,
are complete.

Dedication

This book is dedicated to my husband,
Thomas G. Newman.

He rightly predicted, in December 1978,
that quilting would take over my whole life.
He builds shelves, puts in light bulbs, programs
the computer, shows my quilts in his office, and
encourages my efforts in the quilting business.
His only complaint is that when one "toe
needle" (straight pin) remains in the carpet,
his will be the toe that bleeds!

Thank you, dear, for your infinite patience.

Contents

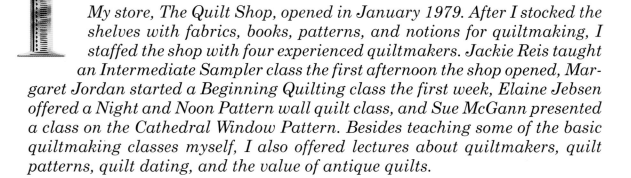

Introduction

My store, The Quilt Shop, opened in January 1979. After I stocked the shelves with fabrics, books, patterns, and notions for quiltmaking, I staffed the shop with four experienced quiltmakers. Jackie Reis taught an Intermediate Sampler class the first afternoon the shop opened, Margaret Jordan started a Beginning Quilting class the first week, Elaine Jebsen offered a Night and Noon Pattern wall quilt class, and Sue McGann presented a class on the Cathedral Window Pattern. Besides teaching some of the basic quiltmaking classes myself, I also offered lectures about quiltmakers, quilt patterns, quilt dating, and the value of antique quilts.

During the first few weeks, it became apparent that the shop could offer still another service. Many customers came in with unfinished quilt blocks and tops started by family members. They hoped to find a seamstress to complete these projects and preserve a bit of their family history.

One of the first projects the seamstresses on my staff and I completed was an identical pair of twin-size Star quilts. Made in the 1930s, the quilts were in perfect condition, heavily quilted, and complete except for binding. In the limited selection of yellow cotton solids on the new fabric shelves was a perfect match. Sewing the bindings on those two quilts was the beginning of a quiltmaking service that has kept us busy ever since. Each year more people bring wonderful vintage blocks and treasured pieces to us for advice, help, encouragement, or completion. Many different projects require the same advice, which inspired me to write this book.

I hope to encourage the continued preservation of our quiltmaking heritage by introducing you to the pleasures of working on vintage quilts, blocks, and tops. This book includes detailed instructions for preparing vintage pieces and blocks, including techniques for coping with the challenges they present. Quiltmaking fundamentals will guide you in sewing any of the settings with ease. The several charts included give essential information for your specific treasures from yesteryear.

The quilts included in this book represent many styles and patterns, dating from 1870 to the present. I give complete instructions for several different block settings as well as for three familiar, non-block designs: Lone Star, Grandmother's Flower Garden, and Double Wedding Ring.

Careful planning and preparation are important when working with vintage blocks or quilt tops. With family treasures, you may get setting and finishing clues from other finished quilts by the same person. The setting for Crow's Nest on page 18 was used by one Texas quiltmaker for two other quilts.[1]

A bit of research into the quilt styles of the period in which the blocks were made ensures the integrity of the quilt you make from the antique blocks. Historical notes appear throughout this text to aid in making the decisions required while planning the authentic completion of your family (or collected) keepsakes.*

A special bonding occurs when you make a quilt from blocks sewn by your mother, grandmother, or other relative. The colors and prints, the particular quilt pattern chosen, and the quality of the work subtly tell you about the one who handled those pieces first. I experience a similar phenomenon while finishing blocks for my shop's customers. After measuring all thirty blocks of a set and finding no two are the same size, I can guess why that quiltmaker put the project away.

An outline containing information about quilt styles from before 1800 to the present begins on page 12. Use it to determine what style of setting and what kind of borders would suit your vintage blocks.

One of my favorite quilt projects was a set of Grandmother's Fan blocks. All the blocks had the same yellow print "handle," but the fan pieces were made from scraps of blue prints in one block, red in another block, and so on. I listed how many blocks of each color I had to work with and set the rows almost effortlessly in a diagonal arrangement with one gray block in the corner, two yellow blocks next, three green blocks, and so on. I've always felt the setting was the original quiltmaker's plan.

Traditionally, unfinished quilt tops and blocks are handed down within families from one generation to the next. However, renewed interest in quiltmaking has led some quilters to collect old, unfinished quilt blocks and tops from other sources. Finishing these pieces of history will not only preserve the tradition of quiltmaking, but will also better preserve the blocks and quilt tops themselves. Finished quilts usually receive better care than unfinished blocks. Whether you inherit or collect vintage pieces, preserving past quiltmaking efforts with integrity is a satisfying quiltmaking endeavor.

***Grandmother's Fan**, Nannie Belle Kent Bryan, circa 1930, Texas. Typical 1930s prints and coordinating solids with blocks set in diagonal rows by color. Collection of Flora and H. R. Bryan.*

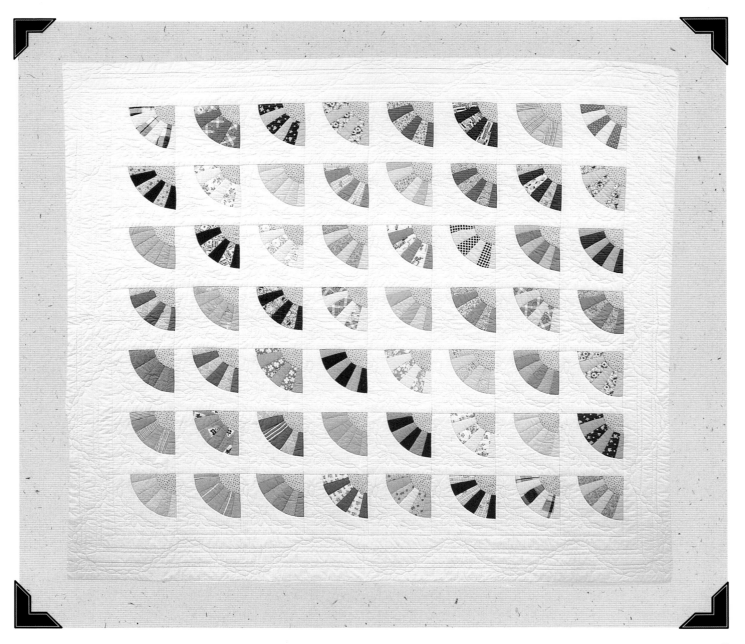

Preparing Vintage Blocks and Fabrics

The first question to answer with old blocks or pieces for quilts is, Will the fabric withstand the work? There is no merit to spending time sewing old fabric that cannot be washed and pressed. The condition of the vintage pieces depends somewhat on how they have been stored. Look carefully at your vintage blocks or pieces. If you are going to spend time and money to finish a vintage quilt project, make sure that the pieces are in workable condition.

Washing Vintage Fabric

Before going far in planning the design for a set of blocks or pieces of blocks, gently wash the fabrics. Orvus® and Ensure are products you can safely use with vintage fabrics. Always test for colorfastness. Use a cotton swab moistened with cool water to rub a particular fabric gently. If color shows on the swab, dye will be lost in washing. Test every color. If no color loss shows on the swab, prepare a solution of warm water and soap in a sink or bathtub. Moisten the swab in the washing solution and test the colors again. Some dyes are released by detergents. Test all the colors. Red and most dark colors from all time periods are likely to run. Even yellow can be a problem.

When you have confirmed colorfastness, put the blocks or pieces in the wash one at a time. By washing one at a time, you will be able to determine the condition of each block or piece. Do not be surprised if a tested color suddenly runs. A fabric that continues to bleed must be removed from the project. Change the washing solution when the dye becomes noticeable. Wash yardage or large remnants of vintage fabric in the same manner as for pieces or blocks.

Rinse each piece, one at a time, in cool water. Rinse at least three times. To prevent strain on the old fabrics and stitches, do not lift the pieces from the wash water. Instead, leave your vintage piece in the sink or bathtub after pulling the drain plug. Press gently to remove the excess water.

Lay the blocks out flat on a towel or an old sheet. As the pieces start to dry, gently shape and finger-press them. While they are damp, it is fairly easy to "square up" blocks. Press, don't iron aggressively. Take care to adjust seam allowances on the backs of the blocks for the flattest appearance possible and for ease in quilting later. Note and mark any unsewn seams for restitching. Add body to limp fabric with fabric sizing. Do not use starch, which attracts insects.

If the fabric in the blocks puckers, the seams draw up, or a disaster occurs, make a new plan for the pieces. If there are permanent stains or holes, decide whether you can tolerate them in the project. I avoid holes, but small stains don't offend me. Use the problem fabric pieces or blocks for repairs and replacement in other blocks. You may want to take apart a misshapen block, cut it with accurate templates, and restitch a better block.

Changing Backgrounds

Quiltmakers usually strive to use the best quality fabrics possible when they make a quilt. In the past, some thin, gauzy muslin was all that was available for block backgrounds. This fabric often appears in the popular Sunbonnet Sue blocks. It may also be found in blocks made from the Dresden Plate and Grandmother's Fan patterns.

Blocks made with this poor-quality muslin background feel so flimsy that you know the fabric will not support any additional work. Often the gauzy background can be changed to a sturdier muslin or solid-color background. Wash the blocks to determine if the appliqués are sturdy enough. You can preserve the better parts of the blocks and, with stable backgrounds, these treasures will make special quilts. See the steps on page 7 to replace the background of an appliquéd block.

Replacing Sunbonnet Sue Backgrounds

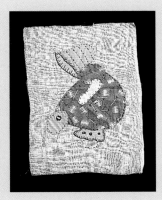

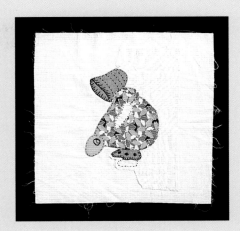

Details on Sunbonnet Sue appliqués are sometimes embroidered on the background fabric. Use the following technique to avoid losing embroidered details when you cut away the background.

1. Use tracing paper to copy embroidered details from the background fabric. Note colors and types of embroidery stitches used.

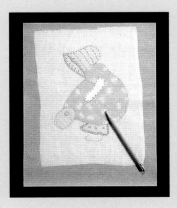

5. Redraw the embroidery details on the new background. Embroider, matching colors and stitches to the original.

6. Place the blocks right side down on a terry-cloth towel and press.
7. Use the renewed blocks in any quilt setting.

2. Cut new background blocks the desired size.
3. Leaving a ⅜" seam allowance, trim the thin background fabric from the appliqué.
4. Position the appliqué on the new background and turn under the old background fabric as you blindstitch the appliqué in place.

⊠⊠⊠⊠⊠⊠⊠⊠ ⊠ **NOTE** ⊠⊠⊠⊠⊠⊠⊠⊠⊠

If embroidery floss was used to appliqué Fans, Dresden Plates, or Sunbonnet Sue figures with buttonhole or running stitches, take care not to snip the floss. Turn under the old background fabric with your needle, allowing old embroidery stitches on the edges to remain on top.

⊠⊠⊠⊠⊠⊠⊠⊠⊠⊠⊠⊠⊠⊠⊠⊠⊠⊠⊠⊠⊠⊠

Sizing Vintage Quilt Blocks

This section includes several proven methods for achieving consistency in the size of your vintage quilt blocks. When you measure your quilt blocks, you may find that the blocks are all the same strange size, such as 9⅝", or some other curious measure. It is more likely, however, that the blocks within a given set are of several different sizes. Bringing all the vintage quilt blocks to the same size will make assembling the quilt much easier.

Consider the pattern of your blocks and the amount of variation in the block sizes. Review all the following methods and choose the one that is adaptable to the most blocks in your set.

Template Sizing

1. Measure all the blocks in a set to identify the largest and smallest ones.

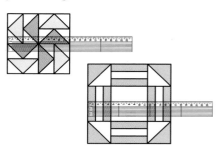

2. If the variance in the block sizes is small, decide on a finished size that accommodates the most blocks.
3. Cut a template the desired finished block size and mark around the template on all the blocks. The marked lines will be the seam lines for the block.

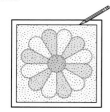

4. Sew the blocks together on the marked lines to produce a tidy top with blocks all the same size and uneven seam allowances concealed on the back. This method sometimes "nips" the sharp points on stars and triangles, but the eye will accept that more readily than the crooked settings that result from odd-size blocks.

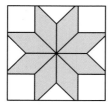

Star points "nipped"

The Crow's Nest blocks on page 18 measured consistently either 8" or 8½", so the quilt contains alternate rows of blocks of the two sizes. The 8" blocks were all marked with one template, and the larger blocks were marked with a template ½" larger.

When the variation in the block sizes is considerable, use one of the following block-sizing methods to adjust the size.

Framing Techniques

A simple way to size blocks is to frame them with fabric. The finished blocks will all be the same size; only the framing widths will differ. Make frames with straight-cut or mitered corners. (See the Stars and Ninepatches quilt on page 48.)

Straight-Cut Frames
1. Measure all the blocks and decide on a larger measurement that allows for a ¾"- to 1½"-wide finished fabric frame around all of the blocks.
2. Cut framing strips on the lengthwise grain of the fabric.
3. Position top edges of blocks on a framing strip as shown, right sides together, and stitch with a ¼"-wide seam. Press the seam toward the block.

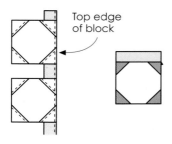

Top edge of block

4. Cut the blocks apart, making sure corners are square.

5. Position the bottom edge of each block on a framing strip and stitch. Press and cut blocks apart.

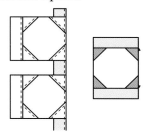

6. Sew framing fabric to the two remaining sides in the same fashion.

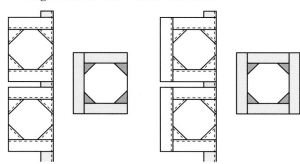

7. Using a square acrylic ruler, trim all the blocks to the measurement determined in step 1.

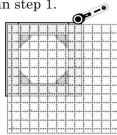

Sizing framed block

Mitered Frames

Mitered corners are especially effective for framing blocks when you use a striped fabric. Alternate the colors of the frames on adjacent blocks for a setting regularly used in 1920s and 1930s quilts.

Mitered frame

1. Measure all the blocks and decide on a larger measurement that allows for a ¾"- to 1½"-wide finished fabric frame around all of the blocks.

2. Cut framing strips of the desired width. Cut the strips the length of the block plus a little more than twice the width of the frame (plus ½" for seam allowances). For example, if the block is a 9" square and the frame will be 2" wide, cut the strips 2½" x 14".

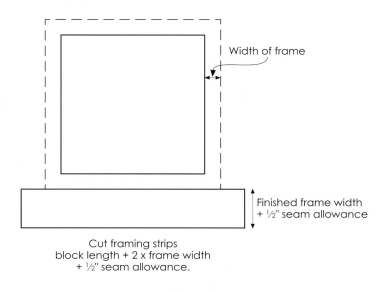

Width of frame

Finished frame width + ½" seam allowance

Cut framing strips
block length + 2 x frame width
+ ½" seam allowance.

⊠⊠⊠⊠⊠⊠⊠⊠⊠⊠ **NOTE** ⊠⊠⊠⊠⊠⊠⊠⊠⊠⊠

If you use striped fabric, plan the width of the frame to fit within the print repeat.

⊠⊠⊠⊠⊠⊠⊠⊠⊠⊠⊠⊠⊠⊠⊠⊠⊠⊠⊠⊠⊠⊠⊠⊠⊠

3. Center the framing strip on the edge of the block with right sides together. Begin stitching ¼" in from the block edge, backstitching at that point. Sew the framing strip to the block, stopping ¼" from the other edge and backstitching. Sew the other three strips to the block in the same way. Press the seam allowances toward the frame.

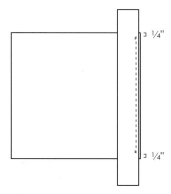

¼"

¼"

Backstitch ¼" from edges.

Mark 45° line on framing strips.

4. Fold the block in half diagonally with right sides together and raw edges matching. Pin to keep the edges together. Use a ruler with a 45° angle to make a line from the seam intersection at the corner of the block to the edge of the strips.

5. Pin on the marked line. (If you are using striped fabric, open the block to make sure that the stripes match.)

6. Begin sewing at the corner of the block where the seams intersect; backstitch. Sew to the outer edge of the framing strips and backstitch. Open the block and check the miter with a square ruler to make sure it really is square and lies flat. Press the seam open.

¼"

7. Trim the excess from the strips, leaving a ¼"-wide seam.

Oval and Circular Frames

To cope efficiently with blocks that are many sizes, or blocks in which the designs are positioned unevenly, place the blocks within a circular or cameo-shaped opening, centered in either a square or rectangle. (See Colonial Ladies on page 53 and Cameo Tulips on page 56).

1. Measure the dimensions of the design to be centered. On graph paper, draft a circle or oval large enough to accommodate the design. (See "Drafting an Oval" on page 11.) Cut out the shape to use as a template.

2. Determine the size of the square or rectangular block that will surround the circular or oval opening. Cut the required number of blocks from background fabric.

3. Center the template for the opening on the right side of the background block

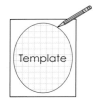

and draw lightly around the circle or oval with a pencil.

Template

4. Position the vintage block, centering the design behind the traced opening. Pin the block and overlaid background fabric together in several places.

5. Inside the traced opening, cut the framing fabric for an inch or two, leaving a ¼"-wide seam allowance. Be careful not to cut the design block behind the framing fabric.

6. Turn under the cut edge just enough to hide the pencil marking. Blindstitch the framing fabric to the design block. Continue cutting an inch or so ahead of the stitching. Do not cut the entire opening at once as it will stretch out of shape.

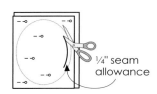

¼" seam allowance

Cut inside the frame marking.

Turn under and blindstitch the cut section.

7. With certain blocks you may wish to layer some of the design outside of the opening onto the framing fabric. (See Cameo Tulips on page 56.) Cut around the part of the design to go outside the opening, leaving a ¼"-wide seam allowance of the background fabric. Clip the background fabric where it intersects with the framing fabric. Turn under the background seam allowance and blindstitch the design to the framing fabric.

Clip around tulip with ¼" seam allowance. Pull to outside of frame and blindstitch.

Drafting an Oval

1. Determine the length and width of the oval that you require. On graph paper or template material, draw two perpendicular lines and, from the point of their intersection, mark half the desired length of the oval on each side of the center on the vertical line. Mark half the width of the oval on each side of the center on the horizontal line.

2. Set a compass to the measure of half the desired oval length (OB). With the point of the compass on the horizontal line at point A, mark the points where the compass intersects the vertical line (C).

3. Place the drawing on a soft surface and place pins on the vertical line at Points C and a pin at one width marker (A). Tie string tightly around the three pins.

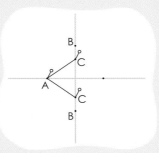

Put a pencil in place of the pin on the horizontal line. Keeping the string taut, draw an oval.

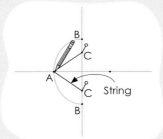

4. Make the rectangle around the oval large enough to provide a frame for the design in the oval.

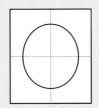

Allow adequate framing fabric around the oval.

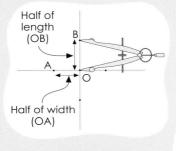

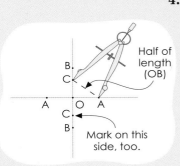

Other Framing Ideas

Use a mitered corner on two sides of a block frame for an Attic Window look. Change the widths of the pieces that form the window for more variations. An additional frame provides greater apparent depth.

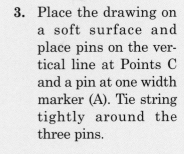

Attic Window Frames

Use a small block as the large center of a Log Cabin–style frame. Use light fabrics on one half and dark on the other.

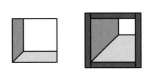

Log Cabin

Appliqué block patterns such as Sunbonnet Sue on page 37 and Butterfly on page 39 are often positioned diagonally on the block. If you use a straight setting, the block design tilts. Sew a triangle to each edge of these on-point blocks to form squares within squares. Then sew them together in straight sets. Refer to the "Side and Corner Triangles" chart on page 81 to determine how large to cut the triangles required for your block.

Small blocks can serve as units in larger block patterns. Combine two, four, or nine small blocks. Arrange the small blocks into Four Patch or Ninepatch blocks and arrange the larger blocks in a suitable setting. See Pattern Quilt 1893–1993 on page 60.

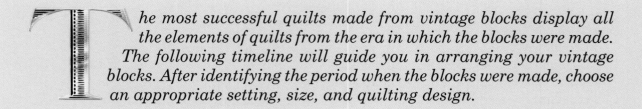

he most successful quilts made from vintage blocks display all the elements of quilts from the era in which the blocks were made. The following timeline will guide you in arranging your vintage blocks. After identifying the period when the blocks were made, choose an appropriate setting, size, and quilting design.

American Quilt Styles

Prior to 1800

Pieced Quilts

Stuffed work and patchwork quilts predominate.
- ✓ Geometric patchwork shapes are common, including hexagons, squares, and triangles, in addition to curved designs such as the clamshell.
- ✓ Tops are heavily quilted in straight lines and grids.
- ✓ Quilts usually do not have borders. Edges are finished with hems or bindings.

Appliqué Quilts

Rarer appliquéd quilts are made of chintz furnishing fabrics and are commonly set in medallion arrangements, with single or multiple chintz borders.
- ✓ Quilts are usually large, from 108" – 144" square.
- ✓ Heavy quilting is featured in circular designs, straight lines, and grids.

1800 to 1840

Medallion Quilts

Medallion quilts are popular. They feature large central patchwork designs, including sunbursts and stars, framed with small patchwork blocks.
- ✓ Quilts are square or rectangular, 100" long or larger.
- ✓ Decorative quilting is featured in backgrounds.

Block-style Quilts

Block-style quilts increase in popularity. Settings feature alternate plain blocks and/or lattices. Patchwork and appliqué designs become smaller to conform to the use of blocks.
- ✓ Quilts have single or multiple straight borders.
- ✓ Patchwork borders of squares, triangles, or diamonds in checkerboard, sawtooth, dog tooth, or other patterns also appear.

One of the earliest published patterns, a honeycomb pattern of patchwork hexagons, is printed in *Godey's Lady's Book and Magazine* in 1835. Typically, heavy quilting outlines the patchwork. Straight lines and grids are also used as quilting designs.

Block-style Quilts

A new trend starts as block quilts are designed for presentation and friendship exchanges. They feature multiple straight borders for increasing the size of joined exchange blocks.

✓ Quilts are either square or rectangular, typically 80"–90" long.
✓ Tops are heavily quilted, in both plain and fancy patterns.

Baltimore Album–style Quilts

Baltimore Album–style quilts from this period are particularly notable. The borders often include appliqué swags with flowers or tassels.

✓ Quilts are square or rectangular, usually 80"–90" long.
✓ Quilts feature heavy quilting in fancy patterns with straight-line or grid background fill.

Block-style Appliqué Quilts

Floral designs are popular through the 1880s; they feature intricate appliquéd borders and complicated quilting patterns of baskets, flowers, feathers, and grids.

Block-style Patchwork Quilts

Alternate-block and lattice settings are common. Quilts have one or more straight borders, or none at all.

✓ Quilting features straight lines and grids, as well as orange-peel and pumpkin-seed motifs.
✓ Geometric patchwork shapes are common.
✓ The Odd Fellow or Charm quilt fad takes hold. Only one piece of many different fabrics is used in these quilts. The quilts have a simple straight border or none at all and feature straight line or outline quilting.

Log Cabin Quilts

Log Cabin designs are developed. These designs are sewn on foundations, using silk, wool, and cotton fabrics. They are rectangular, 80"–90" long. No borders are used; the pattern is worked to the edge of the quilt. There is little or no quilting through the foundation.

Centennial Quilts

Centennial quilts are pieced or appliquéd with patriotic colors and symbols, such as eagles. They are usually set in a medallion style, with either plain or fancy borders. They feature heavy quilting with patriotic motifs, straight lines, and grids.

Victorian Crazy Quilts

This style was prevalent from 1876–1900. Quilters used elegant fabrics and pieced randomly on foundations. Crazy quilts feature fancy embroidery and embellishments and are rarely quilted, being more often tied to backing through the foundation.

1900 to 1920

Appliqué Quilts
Appliqué quilts are uncommon. They have simple frame borders or are bound without borders and feature moderate amounts of straight-line and outline quilting.

Patchwork Block–style Quilts
Patchwork block–style quilts are popular. Patchwork quilts in this period feature seemingly endless variety. Blocks are set straight or diagonally, with alternate blocks and lattice settings.
- ✓ Quilts are rectangular, 75"–90" long.
- ✓ Quilts feature quilting in straight lines and outlines in moderate amounts.

Patriotic Quilts for World War I
These quilts feature:
- ✓ Red, white, and blue solids and prints.
- ✓ Traditional and original patriotic symbols.
- ✓ Quilting in straight lines, outlines, and patriotic motifs.

1920 to 1940

Patterns, fabrics, and settings increase in variety. The most common designs are Double Wedding Ring, Grandmother's Flower Garden, Sunbonnet Sue, Dresden Plate, and Grandmother's Fan. Pastel prints predominate. Borders, rarely used, are generally straight frames, an exception being the curved "ice cream cone" border used on many Dresden Plate quilts and occasionally on other block patterns. Quilt size is typically 72" x 90". Heavy quilting in straight lines, outlines, and grids is common.
- ✓ Floral appliqué medallion quilts introduced by Marie Webster.
- ✓ Designs include borders inspired by the new art styles of the early twentieth century, such as Art Nouveau and Art Deco.
- ✓ Quilts composed of postage-stamp-size pieces become a fad.
- ✓ Embroidered designs and appliqué appear.
- ✓ The first quilt kits become available.

1940 to 1975

Quilts of this period are made using traditional patchwork and appliqué patterns. Cotton fabrics are used when available. Synthetic fabrics contribute to the decline of quiltmaking from 1955–1975.

1975 to Present

Traditional patchwork and appliqué quilt styles are revived. Quilts typically feature intricate patterns and multiple borders. Polyester batting allows for sparse quilting. There is a continually expanding variety in every aspect of quiltmaking. Quilts are made in every size, from tiny wall quilts to king-size bed quilts. "Art quilts" are prevalent. Quilted wearables are increasing in popularity.

Designing Block Settings

After your vintage quilt blocks are washed and sized, you are ready to decide on the style of your quilt. The two main factors involved in planning a quilt setting are the number of usable blocks and the desired size of the finished quilt.

Determine the typical styles of quilts from the period when your vintage blocks were sewn. Refer to the American Quilt Styles timeline on pages 12–14. Play with possible arrangements for your blocks in one of the period styles until you find one you like. Estimate the quilt size. Remember to plan for borders, if desired. Adjust the width of lattice strips and borders to achieve the desired finished quilt size.

Following are a number of traditional settings for quilt blocks and general directions for assembling them.

Side-by-Side Settings

Straight Settings

This is the easiest and most common quilt-block setting. Simply assemble blocks in straight rows.

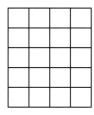

Straight Side-by-Side Setting

1. Make certain all your blocks are the same size. See "Sizing Vintage Quilt Blocks" on pages 8–11.
2. Assemble the blocks in rows and sew them together. Press block seams in one direction in odd-numbered rows and in the opposite direction in even-numbered rows.
3. Sew the rows together, matching block seams and easing in any slight fullness.

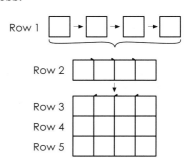

Diagonal Settings

You can also join quilt blocks in a diagonal side-by-side setting. This arrangement is often called "setting blocks on point."

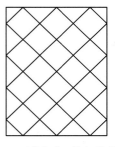

Diagonal Side-by-Side Setting

In planning for this setting, remember that the width of blocks set on point is the diagonal measurement of the block. To calculate the diagonal measurement, multiply the finished side of the square by 1.414.

If you have only a few blocks, a diagonal setting will stretch the size of the quilt you can make with them, especially if you alternate them with plain blocks. Refer to the "Diagonal Settings" chart on page 79 for the number of on-point blocks required for different quilt sizes.

To complete the diagonal setting, use half-square triangles for the sides and quarter-square triangles for the corners. Refer to the "Side and Corner Triangles" chart on page 81 for standard measurements for these side and corner setting triangles.

Cutting Side and Corner Triangles

Cut side and corner setting triangles easily with this "no-math" template method.

1. Cut two squares of template material the finished size of the block.
2. Use one square to mark seam lines on the vintage blocks and cut alternate plain blocks when necessary. Trace around the template on the wrong side of the fabric to mark the sewing line, allowing at least ½" between squares. Cut blocks ¼" outside the marked seam line.

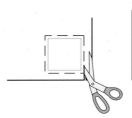

Use one template to mark seam lines on vintage blocks. Cut alternate new blocks.

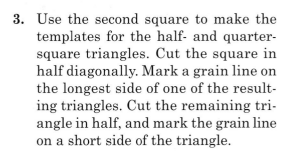

3. Use the second square to make the templates for the half- and quarter-square triangles. Cut the square in half diagonally. Mark a grain line on the longest side of one of the resulting triangles. Cut the remaining triangle in half, and mark the grain line on a short side of the triangle.

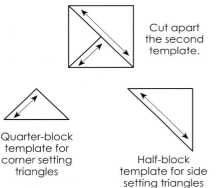

Cut apart the second template.

Quarter-block template for corner setting triangles

Half-block template for side setting triangles

4. On the wrong side of the fabric, position the half-square triangle template, aligning the arrow with the fabric grain line, and trace around it. Cut ¼" from the marked sewing line.

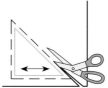

5. On the wrong side of the fabric, position the quarter-square triangle template, aligning it with the fabric grain line, and trace around it. Cut ¼" from the marked sewing line.

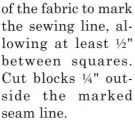

Joining Diagonally Set Blocks

1. Arrange blocks, side setting triangles, and corner triangles in diagonal rows.
2. Join the side setting triangles and blocks in rows. Press seams in one direction for odd-numbered rows and in the opposite direction for even-numbered rows.
3. Sew the rows together, matching the seam intersections and easing as necessary.
4. Sew the corner triangles to the quilt top after joining the rows.

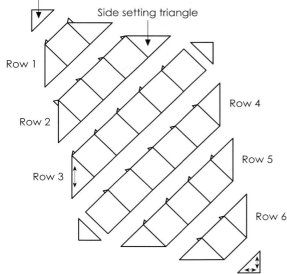

Corner triangle

Side setting triangle

Row 1
Row 2
Row 3
Row 4
Row 5
Row 6

Lattice Settings

Adding lattice strips separates the blocks and enlarges the total project.

Straight Lattice Setting

Diagonal Lattice Settings

Straight Lattice Settings

1. Cut strips the desired lattice width, cutting on the lengthwise grain as shown.

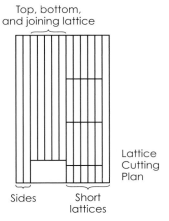

Lattice Cutting Plan

Top, bottom, and joining lattice

Sides Short lattices

2. Reserve enough long strips for the lattice between the rows of blocks. Crosscut the other strips into pieces the length of the block side. See the "Lattice Settings" chart on page 76 for the number of lattice pieces required for various quilt sizes. Sew the short lattice strips between the blocks, forming rows.

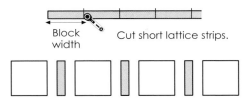

Block width Cut short lattice strips.

Sew blocks and short lattice strips into rows.

3. Before joining rows with long lattice strips, cut strips to the appropriate length. Beginning at one end of a lattice strip, use a pencil to mark the following points on each edge: ¼"-wide seam allowance, finished block width, and so forth, ending with a ¼"-wide seam allowance at the other end. Use these marks to align the blocks accurately from row to row. Mark each long lattice strip.

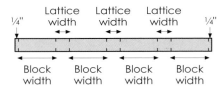

¼" Lattice width Lattice width Lattice width ¼"

Block width Block width Block width Block width

Mark long lattice strips.

4. Pin the marked lattice strip to the row, matching the seams in the rows to the marks on the strip. Stitch.

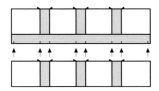

In another variation of the straight lattice setting, rows composed of short lattice strips and cornerstones join the rows of blocks. The cornerstones are small squares cut the same width as the lattice strips so that they line up with the intersections between blocks.

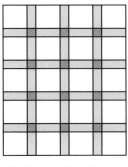

Straight Lattice Setting with Cornerstones

Cornerstones line up with lattice between blocks.

Triple Lattices

When constructing a quilt with a wide lattice (3" or greater), consider dividing the lattice into three strips. The strips may be of equal or unequal widths. This lattice technique makes a quilt more visually interesting, especially when the triple lattice consists of high-contrast colors.

Use straight-cut lattice intersections, as in the Crow's Nest quilt on page 18, or use a plain or pieced square called a cornerstone. The most common pieced cornerstone is the Ninepatch, though quilters also use stars and other patchwork designs.[2]

Quilts from the second half of the nineteenth century exhibit triple lattices, typically in red-and-green or brown-and-pink combinations.[3] Triple lattice quilts at the turn of the century were in black-and-red, navy-and-cream, and red-and-cream combinations. The technique was revived again in the 1930s and quilters employed all possible pastel combinations.[4]

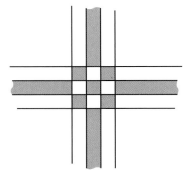

Ninepatch cornerstone for sashing

Crow's Nest

I acquired the forty-two Crow's Nest blocks from another collector who had more projects than she wanted to keep. The blocks measured within ½" of each other, so I template-sized them to either an 8" or 8½" finished size.

The triple lattice design of the sashing accommodates the two block sizes. In the six across and seven down arrangement of the blocks, a row of 8½" blocks measures 59½" and a row of 8" blocks measures 56." The finished width of the triple lattice equals the 3½" difference.

The design involved cutting some of the smaller blocks apart and adding the half-square triangles to the ends of the 8"-block rows. Although it is difficult deciding to cut vintage blocks, it was formerly a common practice in making scrap quilts.

Crow's Nest, *Sharon L. Newman, 1993, Lubbock, Texas, 79" x 92". Triple stripping unifies the blocks in a graphic setting.*

Diagonal Lattice Settings

When planning a diagonally set quilt with a lattice, remember to include the lattice width when calculating the size of side and corner setting triangles. Refer to "Diagonal Settings" on page 15. In some diagonal settings the lattice corners are cut off or, because of the number of rows, corner triangles are unnecessary. See the diagrams of diagonal lattice settings on page 16. Mark the lattice strips as for straight lattice settings.

Medallion Settings

The medallion setting allows flexibility that is useful when designing quilts for vintage blocks. You can frame a large single block with patchwork and borders or join four or more smaller blocks to use as the center medallion. See Fortune Cookie on page 53.

You can easily set vintage pieces and blocks in medallion settings with some advance planning. Use graph paper to plan a setting that features a central unit. Use one large block or join several smaller ones. Add frames, pieced or appliquéd borders, or rows of blocks to achieve the desired quilt size. To see a variety of possible medallion settings, refer to *Sensational Settings* by Joan Hanson (That Patchwork Place).

Churn Dash

I used a medallion setting to plan a design for some vintage Churn Dash blocks. My quilt plan for the blocks is shown at upper right.

The maker—or makers—of the Churn Dash blocks pieced them in three different sizes. Perhaps the first person used the templates to mark seam lines, cutting pieces with a seam allowance all around. The next quilter probably used the templates as cutting-line patterns and made smaller blocks than those in the first set. The third size might have resulted from confusion about the correct size.

Sewing Medallion Settings

1. Measure the central unit, making sure that all corners are square.
2. Add a frame with straight-cut or mitered corners.

3. Attach additional patchwork or appliqué borders. Be consistent with the style of corner you use.

❖❖❖ **TIP** ❖❖❖❖❖❖❖❖❖❖❖❖❖❖❖❖

Work from the center out, measuring and cutting after each addition. Include patchwork blocks or appliqué in your borders if desired.

Medallion Quilts

Medallion-style quilts have been popular with American quiltmakers of several eras. The earliest examples, from the second quarter of the eighteenth century, display parsimonious use of fabrics imported from London and India. In the early nineteenth century, medallion arrangements of central painted or printed designs surrounded by borders evolved into the style known as "broderie perse," in which the quiltmaker cut motifs from the printed fabric and arranged them on a plain background. By the mid-1800s, quiltmakers seldom sewed medallion quilts, opting for the increasingly popular block-style patchwork instead.[5]

Marie Webster led a revival of the medallion style when *The Ladies Home Journal* published four of her appliqué patterns in the January 1911 issue. Webster made her quilts in the newest pastel colors and used original designs. She produced more quilt patterns for the magazine and, in 1915, published the first quilt history book, *Quilts: Their Story and How to Make Them.*

Rose Kretzinger, Dr. Jeanette Throckmorton, and Charlotte Jane Whitehill also gained quiltmaking fame during the 1920s and 1930s with floral appliqué quilts of medallion design.

In the 1920s, The Home Arts Studio published and sold patterns for central medallion designs with borders to frame them. The designs included Gorgeous Chrysanthemum, Giant Dahlia, and Royal Aster.

The commemorative quilts of the American Bicentennial sparked the most recent interest in medallion quilts. Jinny Beyer's award-winning Ray of Light medallion quilt led the way for a new generation of quiltmakers.

Other Settings

Triangles separate vintage blocks in two other traditional settings. Strippy quilts can be designed with single- or multiple-fabric lattices, depending on the proportions of the blocks used. Streak-of-Lightning settings provide a bold look for vintage pieces. The alternating arrangement requires partial blocks and is a good setting for sets of blocks with some partially damaged pieces. Use the good part of partially damaged blocks in the row-end positions.

Sewing Strippy Settings

1. Sew triangles on each edge to set blocks on point.

2. Join blocks in vertical rows.
3. Measure and mark joining strips as you would for lattice strips. (See "Straight Lattice Settings" on page 17.) Stitch and press toward the strip.

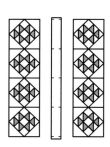 

Mark lattice strip.

Sewing Streak-of-Lightning Settings

1. Size blocks using any method you prefer. (See "Sizing Vintage Quilt Blocks" on pages 8–11.)
2. Cut side setting triangles and corner triangles. (See "Diagonal Settings" on page 15.)
3. Arrange odd-numbered rows using full blocks and adding side triangles in a diagonal arrangement. Add corner triangles to complete rows.

4. Arrange even-numbered rows by beginning and ending with half blocks. (Half blocks must have a ¼"-wide seam allowance on the diagonal edge.) Add half-square triangles in a diagonal arrangement.
5. Mark the center of each side triangle. Join the rows, matching corners of the on-point blocks with the marks on the side triangles.

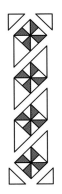
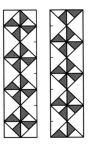

Mark centers of side setting triangles.

Choosing Fabric

Use the best fabric available for your project. New fabrics chosen for use with old blocks should be compatible in color and design. Many reproduction fabrics are available that blend well with vintage pieces. Fabrics come in so many solid colors now that you can often find a match. The new dyes for home hand dyeing are another way to get solid colors that work with vintage pieces.

Vintage fabrics are available in limited amounts. Print yardage and feed sacks from the 1930s are more common than fabric from earlier periods. You may find vintage fabric in pieces that are obviously leftovers from another project. You can determine whether odd pieces provide enough yardage if you have planned your project in advance.

Calculating Yardage

Once you have planned the setting for your vintage pieces, you must determine how much additional fabric to purchase. Using some logical steps, even the most reluctant quilt mathematician can calculate fabric requirements!
1. Make a list, by color and number, of the pieces needed.
2. For each piece, determine how many times it can be cut across the fabric width. (Sometimes the print or stripe in the fabric determines whether to cut pieces lengthwise or across the fabric.) Consider borders and backings first, as they require the most fabric. Don't forget fabric for binding.
3. Determine how many rows of a particular piece you must cut.
4. Multiply the number of rows by the width of the row. The result is the amount of fabric required for that particular piece.
5. Add the measurements obtained in step 4 for each piece to find the total amount of fabric you need.

A sketch of the cutting plan is helpful, and a quarter-yard of "insurance fabric" is worth every penny.

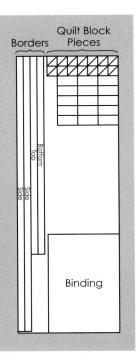

aking Quilts from Vintage Pieces

Three popular old quilt patterns are not pieced in blocks, but sewn in units. These units are often left unfinished. The Double Wedding Ring may be found in pieces shaped something like footballs or circles, the hexagonal Grandmother's Flower Garden is typically abandoned after the basic flower units are sewn, and the Lone Star design is often found in diamond-shaped pieces joined without background fabric. Following are directions for completing each of these classic quilt designs.

Double Wedding Ring

The origin of this beloved twentieth-century pattern is not well documented. Double Wedding Ring quilts were extremely popular during the 1930s. Hundreds of them were made of pastel prints set on muslin backgrounds with pink and green setting squares, exactly as described in the weekly newspaper patterns.

One day in 1981, a package came to The Quilt Shop with postage due. The package was bulging with pieced Double Wedding Ring bands—enough for a quilt. There was no return address, no name inside, no way to know who had sent them trusting that someone in a quilt store would know what to do with the bands!

I drafted a version of the Double Wedding Ring pattern to fit the bands and made templates. The quilt is still in progress, and I use the pieces to demonstrate the steps for sewing the units and assembling a Double Wedding Ring quilt.

In the late 1920s, in Brown County, Texas, Bessie Sawyer carefully cut ninety-four curved bands of paper from pages of the 1928 and 1929 Sears Roebuck and Montgomery Ward catalogs. Using scraps from her recent dressmaking efforts, she pieced fabric to fit the bands. She planned to have a Double Wedding Ring quilt sewn together before the wedding she dreamed she would have someday.

When she moved west to Scurry County, Bessie continued adding pieces from her home-sewn clothing to the bands.

Thomas Jackson Newman was the young man in the neighborhood who drove all the young people to the community events and dances. He began to court Bessie. He even came to sit by the fireplace, watching her sew, and handing her scraps as she worked on her quilt. Bessie and Thomas married in October 1931.

The busy nature of a new marriage in the early years of the Depression kept progress on the Double Wedding Ring quilt slow. Bessie added bits of fabric from the rompers she sewed for their first son, born in 1933.

Around 1936, Bessie completed the last of the paper bands. Time to assemble the quilt was hard to find as the family grew to include four sons, and Thomas's job required frequent family moves. Bessie had also started a Puppy Dog appliqué quilt and a Many Trips Around the World in postage-stamp-size pieces for the two oldest boys. Warm quilts with simple designs and easy quilting she finished and put to use. The Postage Stamp quilt was finally finished when the second son was forty-eight years old. The Puppy Dog quilt was completed and given to the first son after fifty-two years.

Through the years, Bessie often showed the Double Wedding Ring bands to daughters-in-law and granddaughters. "I'm going to put those together with red and fill in the edge to be straight," she said. In 1992, she realized that she was too busy to finish the Double Wedding Ring quilt. She gave me, her third daughter-in-law, permission to complete the quilt.

Because of the fragile nature of the vintage fabrics in the bands, this quilt is sparsely quilted. Only one line of quilting curves through the bands and extends through the squares, interlocking in large circles. Quilting in the center fabric outlines the bands. The loop design in the centers is consistent with the amount of quilting on the bands. The curves quilted in the straight-edge pieces echo the curves in the bands.

The ninety-four bands Bessie string-pieced were finally joined into a Double Wedding Ring quilt. It was completed in time for the Newmans' sixty-second wedding anniversary.

Double Wedding Ring, Bessie Sawyer Newman and Sharon Hicks Newman, 1928–1993, Lubbock, Texas, 70" x 82". Red has been used in every one of Bessie's quilts and certainly sets off the pastel wedding ring bands well. Note the additional pieces filling out the curved edges.

Drafting Wedding Ring Templates

Because curved piecing requires very accurate seaming in order to lie flat, the Double Wedding Ring can best be completed using templates. The hardest part of completing an unfinished Double Wedding Ring is obtaining or re-creating the patterns for the oval and center if they are not included with the pieced bands. The arc of the band is critical to the finished shape of the pattern.

Hundreds of patterns have been printed, copied, and shared because of the popularity of this pattern. The number of pieces in the bands may be as few as four or as many as a dozen, and the connecting pieces may or may not be exact squares. The older patterns had wider bands than current ones and, often, the shape of the older ring was more square than round. The many variations possible in the different parts of the pattern make finding an exact match with a printed pattern unlikely.

Drafting the ring in a finished size is easiest if only the bands are pieced and the ovals and centers have not been cut. Use the band as a starting point and draft a ring that allows the band template to be marked on the actual patchwork, leaving seam allowances all around. Make sewing-line templates for the oval and center (without seam allowances).

Template for band
that will fit on vintage band

Joining the Pieces

Arlene Stamper of San Diego, California, developed a method of piecing the Double Wedding Ring units that makes the assembly easier than with previous methods. Use the chart on page 81 to compute the number of pieces needed. Celebrate when the top is sewn together!

1. Mark the sewing lines on the bands, ovals, and ring centers. Add registration marks for matching the centers of the ovals, bands, and each side of the center fabric.

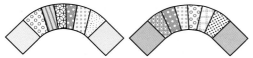

Band   Oval

Center

2. Sew a band to one edge of the oval. Make two of these "melon" units. Press the seam away from the background fabric.

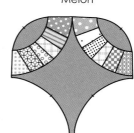

Melon

3. Sew a melon to each of two adjacent sides of a center, creating a clamshell-shaped unit. Press the seams toward the bands. Prepare all the centers this way.

4. Sew a connecting square from one fabric to each end of half of the remaining pieced bands. Use the other connecting fabric for squares at each end of the remaining bands.

Sew the same fabric to each end of bands.

5. Join pairs of bands to form a rainbow. Make the same number of rainbows as centers.

Join bands to
make rainbows.

6. With the rainbow arc combination on top, sew all the rainbow arcs to the clamshells sewn in step 3.

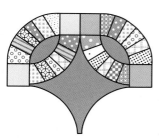

Clamshell with Rainbow

7. Join the remaining bands and ovals to make football-shaped units. Use one connecting fabric for half of the blocks and another connecting fabric with the other half.

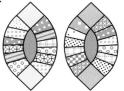

Football units for completing edges

8. Place the pieced units in diagonal rows. The curved edges of each clamshell fits into place with the next one in the row. Be sure to match registration marks on bands and center pieces, as well as the seams where the football units meet. Add single squares to create a scalloped edge, if desired.

9. Following the numbers on the illustration below, join the units one by one, row by row. Press seam allowances toward the pieced bands.

10. To complete the pattern with a straight edge rather than the traditional scalloped edge, draft templates for the edge unit and corner. Assemble as shown.

Follow these steps for better results when stitching a Double Wedding Ring band to a center piece. This technique ensures accurate intersections that don't come apart and prevents you from accidentally backstitching off the seam line.

1. Pin the sharp corner of the center piece to the band, matching the seam intersections exactly.
2. Begin sewing ½" away from the edge of the fabric.
3. Sew to end of the seam line. With the needle down, turn the work around, sew over the stitches just sewn and back to the other end of the band.
4. With the needle down, lift the presser foot and turn the work around again. Sew back about ½" over the previous line.

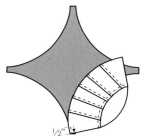

Begin stitching ½" from end of seam.

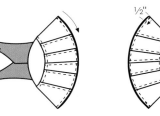

Turn and sew to end of band.

Turn and sew ½" over previous stitching.

❖❖❖❖❖❖❖❖❖❖❖❖❖❖❖❖❖❖❖❖❖❖❖

Finishing

Refer to "Finishing Vintage Quilts" on pages 65–74.

1. Press the finished quilt top and mark the quilting design.
2. Layer the quilt top with batting and backing. Baste and quilt.
3. Bind the edges.
4. Sign and date your Double Wedding Ring quilt.

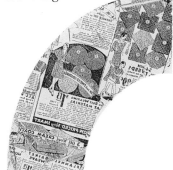

Quilt Patterns
String Pieced on Paper

Collectors of antique quilt blocks find many patterns stitched on paper by machine and, surprisingly, some sewn to the paper foundation by hand. The triangles in the Double Pinwheel quilt on page 46 were machine stitched on newsprint. The bands for the Double Wedding Ring on page 23 were hand stitched on catalog pages.

What fun to read the news of the past and compare prices with those of today! The dilemma is how to preserve the vintage printed matter and finish the project too.

To preserve history, photocopy the printed backing while it is still attached to the fabric. The copy will probably be more readable than the yellow newspaper. (See 1898 Stars in Garden Maze on page 50). Remove the paper backing by gently pulling the paper against the seams. Use a seam ripper to get the paper started where necessary. You may want to photocopy some of the reverse sides of the newspapers also.

Mark any broken stitches you find while removing paper and repair them before washing the project.

Numerous string-pieced quilt patterns developed from quilters' efforts to use small scraps of fabric efficiently. Paper shapes create foundations for stitching and folding small pieces of fabric into place, ensuring uniformity and stability for the pieces.

Thrifty quiltmakers have used these string-piecing techniques for a long time, as evidenced by examples from the 1890s, 1920s, 1930s, and 1940s. Contemporary quiltmakers are reviving the technique. Shapes such as squares, triangles, and diamonds are the most common string-pieced patterns. (See 1898 Stars in Garden Maze and Double Pinwheel.) However, other more unusual shapes can also be string pieced, such as the 1928 Double Wedding Ring and the 1930s Fortune Cookie on page 53.

Sewing String-Pieced Patchwork

1. Cut identical paper shapes, such as squares, diamonds, or triangles. Traditionally, quilters have used newspaper, catalog, or magazine pages, but any lightweight paper will do.
2. Set the machine stitch length to 12 stitches per inch. Use a sharp needle. Stitch some paper to a fabric scrap to be sure you can remove the paper easily with the stitches intact.
3. Use narrow scraps of fabric. Position the first piece right side up across the center of the paper. (See illustrations below.)
4. Place the next scrap on the first with right sides together and one edge matched.
5. Stitch a ¼"-wide seam through the paper and both fabrics.
6. Open the second scrap flat on the paper and press. Continue adding strips to both sides of the center. Make sure to open each seam completely so no tucks are stitched in the next seam.
7. When the paper is covered, trim the fabric scraps even with the edge of the paper.

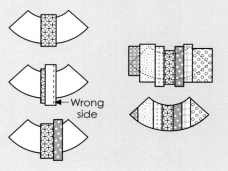

Grandmother's Flower Garden

Hexagons in Patchwork

Quiltmakers have been sewing the hexagon into a variety of designs for centuries. The honeycomb pattern, published in *Godey's Lady's Book* in January, 1835, was adapted from nature, and has been interpreted in silk and wool, as well as cotton.

The earliest samples date from the mid-nineteenth century and were sewn in the English patchwork method of basting the patches over paper hexagons and then "whipping" the pieces together.

You must cut stacks and stacks of pieces to make even a small Grandmother's Flower Garden quilt. A single flower unit of three fabrics contains nineteen hexagons. There are even more hexagons in the joining rows. No wonder so many of these quilts remain unfinished!

During the 1930s, hundreds of Flower Garden quilts were pieced and quilted with stitching "by the piece"—that is, quilting ¼" away from the edge of every hexagon. But even more Flower Garden quilts remained at some stage short of completion.

Often, collectors find flower units neatly stacked in a box along with the hexagon pattern for cutting the joining rows. Sometimes, a section of the top is assembled, giving an idea of the setting arrangement the maker originally planned. Occasionally, the top is pieced but unquilted.

Margaret Reid acquired many hexagons that were already cut, strung together in stacks, and stored in a sugar sack. Margaret's mother-in-law, Ouida Campbell Reid, gave her the collection. Amanda Campbell, grandmother of Margaret's husband, Bill, had cut most of the hexagons from scraps of his baby clothes. The little conversation prints are coordinated with pastel solids.

Margaret joined the hexagons in flower and diamond shapes and appliquéd them into wall quilts for her four grandchildren. She labeled each with the name of the children's great-great-grandmother, who started the quilts, and her own name, the one who preserved and completed them.

1.

2.
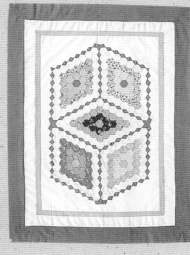

3.

4.

5.
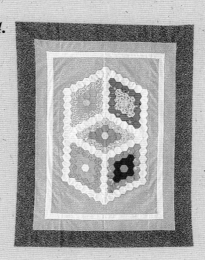

1. Rings. Nineteen hexagon flowers, each outlined in muslin, are joined in a hexagonal arrangement with pieced diamonds and triangles forming concentric rings of different colors.

2. Flower Garden, 37½" x 38½." Hexagon flowers, arranged in rows of 2, 3, and 2, are separated by one row of muslin hexagons. More muslin hexagons fill out the flowers to a "square."

3. Boxes, 33" x 44." Diamond Field units are created by adding two extra hexagons on opposite sides of the usual flower unit. Muslin hexagons outline the flowers, and diamonds and triangles join the pieced diamonds in a 2/1/2 arrangement.

4. Dark Boxes, 29½" x 39." Diamond Field units joined with muslin hexagons are appliquéd on a blue background.

5. Spokes, 39½" x 40½." Flower units pieced with a center, two solid or print rows, and one row of muslin hexagons are set 2/3/2 using diamonds and tiny triangles. The arrangement is appliquéd on a muslin background.

Flower Garden, *Inez Adams, 1990, Lubbock, Texas. Quilted by The Quilt Shop. When the first reproductions of 1930s fabrics were printed, Inez Adams purchased a set of quarter-yard pieces with all the available colors and prints. She had a flower garden quilt precut for consistency in the hexagons and arranged the flowers in a pattern of vertical rows of flowers separated by yellow-centered diamonds.*

Drafting a Hexagon Template

Use a compass to draw a hexagon template the size of your pieces. Draw your pattern on paper, then trace it onto template plastic.

1. Set the radius of the compass to measure half the diameter of the finished hexagon from point to point. Draw a circle.

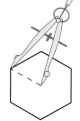

Measure hexagon. Set compass at ½ hexagon diameter.

Draw circle.

2. Place the point of the compass on the circle and draw an arc, intersecting the circle twice. Move the point of the compass to an intersection and continue drawing arcs in this fashion around the circle.

Draw arcs around circle.

3. To form the hexagon, join the intersection points with straight lines.

Connect arc intersections.

4. Draw around the hexagon template on fabric, adding ¼"-wide seam allowances on all sides before cutting.

Stitching the Flowers

You can hand stitch hexagons for the traditional flower-garden units without stopping if you don't mind a little repeat stitching. Basting back over the short seam is faster than tying off and making new knots for each individual seam.

1. Stitch two hexagons together along one side, leaving ¼" free at each end. (One piece will be the center hexagon.)
2. Add a hexagon, stitching from the seam between the original two hexagons outward.
3. Baste back along the seam just sewn, and then stitch the seam joining the next hexagon to the center. Stitch each hexagon you add to its neighbor before stitching it to the center hexagon.

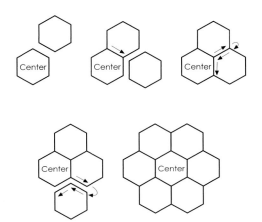

Planning a Flower Garden Setting

Use hexagon graph paper to plan quilts made from this intriguing shape. Because of their shape, hexagons fit together in uneven rows. An odd number of rows forms the most symmetrical arrangement.

To enlarge the setting of flower shapes, consider adding a row of hexagons around each flower and joining the units with green diamond shapes. The green diamonds represent the "garden path" to some quiltmakers and the "vine" between flowers to others. The tiny triangle necessary in this setting represents a bud and was often a pink fabric. Pyramids of green hexagons can also be used between the flower units to represent leaves.

Finishing the Edges

Because the outer edge of a Grandmother's Flower Garden quilt is so irregular, a binding requires many miters and is most easily applied in a single thickness, as narrow as a scant ⅜". Trimming Flower Garden quilt edges to a smooth curve was a common practice in the 1930s. Some quiltmakers trimmed a straight edge for the quilt right through the blocks. Often, the top and bottom were left with gentle curves and the sides cut straight. To attach a border to a Flower Garden quilt without cutting off the flowers, turn under the ¼"-wide seam allowance on each hexagon and appliqué the quilt-top edge to a border strip of the desired width.

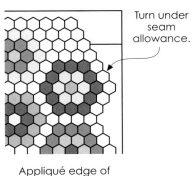

Turn under seam allowance.

Appliqué edge of quilt top to border.

Conversation Prints

Conversation prints are the tiny designs, such as the horseshoes, insects, and sewing implements, printed on fabric during the last quarter of the nineteenth century. The prints in production from 1915 into the mid-1930s included designs for children that featured bears, bunnies, mice, and seemingly every other animal. Some of the prints were illustrations of Victorian children by Kate Greenaway. Other novelty designs included brooms and mops, nursery rhyme and farm scenes (used in the Double Wedding Ring quilt on page 23), as well as country, circus, and other themes.

Lone Star

After Four Patch and Ninepatch quilts, star designs have been the most popular patterns throughout quilt-making history. The eight points on a center square of the Variable Star and the eight diamonds of the LeMoyne Star have been adapted into hundreds of designs. Early blocks measured four to nine inches square, while twentieth-century blocks are generally nine to sixteen inches square. (See Stars and Ninepatches on page 48 and 1898 Stars in Garden Maze on page 50.)

Rows of diamonds make up each star point of the large Bethlehem Star. Star designs require "fill in" squares and triangles. Many of the earliest examples of Bethlehem Star quilts are embellished with appliqué, and some have patchwork in the background squares and triangles.

In the early twentieth century, plain background squares and triangles decorated with intricate quilting designs were more common. The name "Lone Star" became popular as the quilt design traveled with quiltmakers west from Pennsylvania.

Kits with diamonds already cut for the stars have been produced for many decades. The quiltmaker chose the background fabric for quilts made from these kits—sometimes light or dark solids, often muslin.

Finishing the Lone Star

Stars are most often left unfinished when all eight diamonds are joined together and the squares and triangles need to be added.

Some quiltmakers have difficulty with the center of the star. Stitching eight diamonds

Hattie Turner Jones pieced the pastel diamonds forming this star. She was in her thirties and living in Homot, Texas, in the early 1930s. Around 1978, Hattie took the star apart and sewed it together again because she knew she could do a better job after years of sewing experience. Her health changed suddenly, and she could not complete the Lone Star quilt. Her daughter, Frances Hambright, commissioned the completion of the project.

The star is positioned so that when the quilt is placed on a bed and tucked over the pillow, the design is fully visible. The cream fabric used to "float" the star gives additional width to the quilt. The solid green border completes the pastel 1930s color scheme.

Lone Star, Texas, 78" x 94". Typical prints of the 1930s can be seen in this eight-pointed, unfinished star. Muslin background and a matching solid green border provide the finishing touches for a guest-bed quilt.

together smoothly requires careful attention to seam lines and care in sewing bias edges.

If your star has a lumpy center:
1. From the center outward, unstitch approximately 6" of the seams between every other star point.
2. Press one two-diamond section and place an 8" Bias Square® ruler on the seam between the two star points. The edges of the diamonds should line up with the edges of the ruler. If they do not, mark a true right-angle sewing line in the seam allowances. Press and mark all four diamond sections.

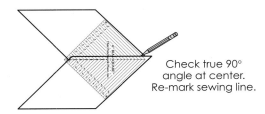

Check true 90° angle at center. Re-mark sewing line.

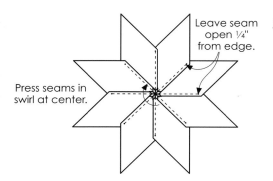

Leave seam open ¼" from edge.

Press seams in swirl at center.

3. Sew the diamonds together, matching the newly marked seam lines and sewing just inside the lines. Press all the seams in one direction, so that they form a swirl around the center.

If you have pieced diamonds that are not joined:

1. Measure the diamonds against each other to see if they vary in size. If the differences are minor (up to ¼"), easing while sewing will accommodate the variance.

2. If the differences are larger than ¼", check the assembly of the diamonds. Even a minor error on the many seams in a Lone Star diamond unit can become a large problem. Unstitch and resew any seam that appears too wide or too narrow.

3. When the eight diamonds are approximately the same size, mark seam lines and join in pairs. If possible, arrange the diamonds so that a bias edge is sewn to a straight edge. Sew with the bias edge on the bottom, and the straight grain on top, right sides together. Stitch from the center point of the star up to ¼" from the outer corner, leaving the seam allowance free for setting in the background squares and triangles later. Press the seam to one side. Make sure that the inside and outside corners of the two-diamond units form right angles.

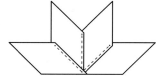

Both corners form right angles.

Stitch to ¼" from each edge.

4. Sew diamond-unit pairs into star halves.

5. Sew halves together, stitching just inside the marked seam lines. Press the seams in one direction, so that they form a swirl. See illustration at the top of the page.

Adding Background Pieces

Once you have a star completed, add the background pieces needed to form a square quilt top.

1. Measure the outer edges of each star point from the point to the seam intersection. Add ¼" for the seam allowance. Note the measurement on a scrap of paper and pin it to that edge. All of the star-point measurements should be the same. On an old star, it may become obvious why the project was abandoned when you discover that all of the measurements are different! If the differences are within ¼" of each other, the longer points can be eased to fit.

2. Cut corner squares the length of the star point plus a ¼"-wide seam allowance.

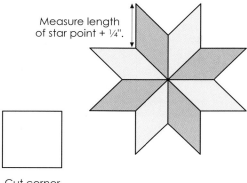

Measure length of star point + ¼".

Cut corner squares length of star point + ¼".

3. Add 1¼" to the star-point length (which includes a ¼"-wide seam allowance). Cut a square this size, then cut the square twice diagonally as shown. (See the "Side and Corner Triangles" chart on page 81.)

Cut squares for side triangles length of star point + ¼" + 1¼".

4. Sew the triangles in place first. Pin the point of the triangle in place at the intersection of the diamonds and con-

tinue pinning to the edge, easing as necessary to match the two edges. Begin stitching ¼" from the inner edge. Sew from the center to the outer point.

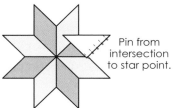

Pin from intersection to star point.

5. Pin the second side of the triangle in place, easing as necessary. Sew from the center to the edge. Continue inserting triangles around the star. Press the seam allowances toward the diamonds.

Sew from inner to outer edge.

6. Pin a corner square to the star with right sides together, matching the seam allowances at the intersection of the diamonds. Ease the edges as necessary. Sew from the inner corner to the tip of the star.

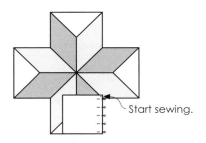

Start sewing.

7. Pin and sew the second side of the square, easing as required.

8. Pin and sew the remaining squares. After the star is filled in with side tri-

angles and corner squares, add borders as desired.

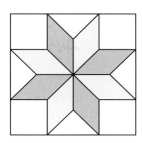

Using Sizing Strips

If the difference in the star point measurements is greater than ¼", sizing strips may be the solution. Cut strips from the same fabric as the background squares and triangles so that the different lengths of the star points won't be noticeable.

1. Cut 2"-wide strips across the 44" width of the fabric. Sew a strip to each side of each point, sewing from the point up to ¼" from the inner edge; backstitch.

2. Press the strips and miter them at the star points and corner intersections. (See "Borders with Mitered Corners" on pages 65–66.)

3. With the star flat on your work surface, measure all of the star points to the tip of the unfinished spacing strips.

4. Mark the length of the shortest star point on the sizing strips of all of the other star points.

5. Using a large Bias Square, trim the sizing strips on the larger star points. The spacing strips will look unevenly trimmed if you trim correctly. Because the sizing strips and background squares and triangles are the same color, the difference in the width of the spacing strips will be not be noticeable and the quilting design will make the spaces around the star look uniform.

6. Cut corner squares and side triangles of background fabric as directed in steps 1–3 on page 32.

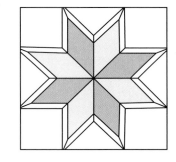

Making Quilts from Vintage Blocks

The quilts in this section contain block sets that are typical of the many unfinished quilts I have encountered. Some of the pictured quilts are accompanied by quilt plans and instructions. Others are included as additional examples of the types of settings that suit vintage blocks. I give exact measurements for the pictured quilts. If your blocks are the same size, you may follow the directions exactly. If your blocks are a different size, consult the charts on pages 75–76 for size, cutting, and yardage information.

Traditional Pieced Alternate Blocks

 Pinwheel

 Octagon

 Square on Point

 Triple Bars

 Half Squares

 Ninepatch

 Puss in the Corner

St. Andrew's Cross

Kay Jackson Fleming collects and documents family quilts and works with local guilds and statewide groups to document historical quilts. She purchased eighteen vintage blocks of an unknown pattern at an estate sale in the 1980s. Kay chose to piece the St. Andrew's Cross pattern for the alternate blocks because the lines were similar to those in the vintage blocks.

In *Historic Quilts,* Florence Peto describes St. Andrew's Cross:

"The St. Andrew's Cross was sure protection against sorcery; a witch placing her hand on a door-knocker into which the occupant of the house had had the foresight to cut a St. Andrew's Cross, would be rendered helpless and impotent. Tools and guns so marked never disappeared or behaved badly."[6]

The same block was later called "Kentucky Chain."

St. Andrew's Cross, *Kay Fleming, 1986, Lubbock, Texas, 74" x 102". This quilt top combines vintage blocks of an unknown pattern with alternate pieced blocks that extend the design elements forming new images.*

Quilt size: 74" x 102"
Block size: 14" x 14"
Number of blocks:
      17 St. Andrew's Cross blocks
      18 Unknown Pattern blocks
Setting: Side by side

Materials
2 yds. (total) assorted medium or dark print
    scraps
6 yds. (total) assorted light prints and solids
    for background
3 yds. dark print for St. Andrew's Cross
    block, border, and binding
6¼ yds. backing fabric

Cutting
Use templates on pages 87–89 to cut
block pieces.

From the scraps, cut:
 18 of Template I
 36 each of Templates J, M, and N
 18 of Template K

From the background fabric, cut:
280 of Template B
136 of Template C
 72 of Template L
 18 of Template H

From the dark print, cut:
 2 border strips, each 2½" x 102½", from
    the length of the fabric
 2 border strips, each 2½" x 70½", from
    the length of the fabric
 34 each of Templates A, A reversed, D, F,
    and G
106 of Template E

St. Andrew's Cross Block

St. Andrew's Cross Block   Unit 1   Unit 2
                          Make 34.   Make 34.

This block consists of two units that
appear to be mirror images of each other
but aren't exactly. The slight difference in
the units creates an interesting woven ef-
fect in the finished block. To piece the block,
join the units in pairs, then join the pairs.

1. Follow the piecing diagrams below to
   make 34 of each unit.

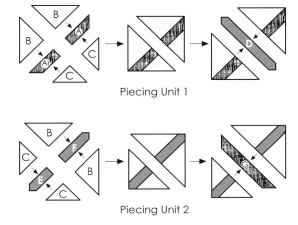

Piecing Unit 1

Piecing Unit 2

2. Join the completed units to make 17 blocks.

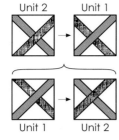

Unknown Pattern

Unknown Pattern

1. Assemble 18 Log Cabin center squares as shown.

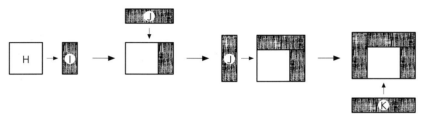

2. Add piece L to opposite sides of each Log Cabin center, then add a piece L to each of the remaining sides.

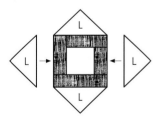

3. Add a piece M to opposite sides of each center unit, then add a piece N to each of the remaining sides.

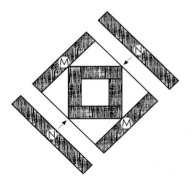

4. Assemble pieced corner triangles as shown.

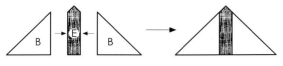

Make 4 for each block.

5. To complete each block, add a pieced corner triangle to each side of the center square.

Quilt Top Assembly

1. Referring to the quilt plan on page 35, arrange the blocks in 7 rows of 5 blocks each.
2. Sew the blocks together in horizontal rows and press the seams in opposite directions from row to row (to the right in odd-numbered rows, to the left in even-numbered rows). Sew the completed rows together, being careful to match seam lines.
3. Sew the top and bottom borders to the quilt top. See "Borders with Straight-Cut Corners" on page 65.
4. Sew the borders to the sides of the quilt.

Finishing

Refer to "Finishing Vintage Quilts" on pages 65–74.
1. Press the finished quilt top and mark the quilting design.
2. Layer the quilt top with batting and backing. Baste and quilt.
3. Bind the edges.
4. Sign and date your St. Andrew's Cross quilt.

Sunbonnet Sue

Sue Caraway wanted a queen-size quilt made from her twenty Sunbonnet girls. Her mother, Mary A. Hicks, began stitching the blocks in Roscoe, Texas, when Sue was a child. Mary cut the dresses for the Sunbonnet girls from scraps left over when she sewed dresses for Sue and her sister, Latrille.

This setting enlarges the 10½" x 10½" Sunbonnet blocks by adding triangles on all four sides. The colors of the triangles alternate in this easy, side-by-side diagonal setting. The triple border adds the necessary width for a queen-size quilt. Using the triangle fabrics in the border gives the finished quilt a coordinated look.

This setting required only eighteen blocks. Two Sunbonnet Sues not included in the quilt were made into ruffled decorator pillows to use with the quilt on a guest bed.

Sunbonnet Sue setting designed by Jackie Reis, 1991, Lubbock, Texas, 84" x 104". This setting was designed to accommodate eighteen blocks in a queen-size quilt. Quilted by The Quilt Shop.

If you wish to make this quilt but do not have any Sunbonnet Sue blocks, there are many classic Sue patterns available.

Quilt size: 83" x 104"
Block size: 14⅞" x 14⅞"
Number of blocks: 18
Setting: Diagonal side by side

Materials

11¾ yds. blue solid for corner triangles, inner and outer borders, backing, and binding
3¾ yds. light print for corner triangles, middle borders, and side and corner setting triangles
18 Sunbonnet Sue blocks, each 10½" x 10½"

Cutting

From the blue solid, cut:
2 strips, each 3½" x 63½", for inner border
2 strips, each 3½" x 90½", for inner border
2 strips, each 3½" x 77½", for outer border

2 strips, each 3½" x 104½", for outer border
24 squares, each 11¾" x 11¾", for block triangles

From the light print, cut:
2 strips, each 4½" x 69½", for middle border
2 strips, each 4½" x 98½", for middle border
12 squares, 11¾" x 11¾", for block triangles
3 squares, 22¼" x 22¼", for side setting triangles
2 squares, 15¾" x 15¾", for corner setting triangles

Sunbonnet Sue Blocks

1. Using the template method, measure and size your Sunbonnet Sue blocks to 10½" x 10½". (See pages 8–11.)
2. Cut each of the twenty-four 11¾" blue squares once diagonally to yield 48 triangles.
3. Cut each of the twelve 11¾" light print squares once diagonally to yield 24 triangles.

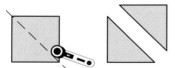

Cut blue solid and light print squares into triangles.

4. Sew blue triangles to each side of 12 Sunbonnet Sue blocks.
5. Sew light print triangles to each side of 6 Sunbonnet Sue blocks.

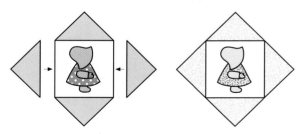

Make 12 blue solid.   Make 6 light print.

Quilt Top Assembly

1. Following the quilt plan, above left, arrange the blocks in a diagonal setting, alternating the Sue blocks framed with blue and those framed with the light print. Place large light-print tri-

angles at the ends of the rows and small light-print triangles at the corners. Join the rows, pressing seams in opposite directions on alternate rows.

2. Sew 3½" x 63½" blue strips to the top and bottom of the quilt top. Add 3½" x 90½" blue strips to the sides.

3. Sew 4½" x 69½" light-print strips to the top and bottom of the quilt top. Add 4½" x 98½" light-print border strips to the sides.

4. Sew 3½" x 77½" blue border strips to the top and bottom. Sew 3½" x 104½" blue strips to the sides, completing the quilt top.

Finishing

Refer to "Finishing Vintage Quilts" on pages 65–74.

1. Press the finished quilt top and mark the quilting design. Outline each Sunbonnet Sue and place hearts or cables in the corner triangles added to the blocks.

2. Layer the quilt top with batting and backing. Baste and quilt.

3. Bind the edges.

4. Sign and date your Sunbonnet Sue quilt.

Butterfly

Joyce Braus found a treasure trove of her grandmother's quilt blocks in the cedar chest left when her mother died. Joyce's mother, Frances, had never liked quilting because she felt she could not meet her mother's exacting standards for small quilting stitches.

Joyce's grandmother, Anna Michulka, was born on October 11, 1873, in Eagle, Texas. In 1891 she married John J. Drapela, an immigrant from Austria-Hungary. They had thirteen children. Joyce's mother, Frances, was the youngest.

Quilting was a constant in Anna's life. She made quilts for daily use, along with a Double Wedding Ring for each son and daughter who married. Anna stopped quilting in the 1940s, after the girls left home, but continued sewing blocks and tops.

Butterfly, blocks circa 1930, by Anna Michulka, Eagle, Texas, 76" x 96". Butterflies set diagonally on blocks remain upright when set with alternating plain blocks in a diagonal setting. Completed by The Quilt Shop, 1989.

The simple diagonal side-by-side setting in this quilt highlights the old-fashioned Butterfly appliqué blocks. A soft peach solid block alternates with the Butterfly blocks made of pastel prints.

Quilt size: 78" x 91"
Block size: 9" x 9"
Number of blocks: 30
Setting: Diagonal side by side

Materials

2 yds. (total) assorted print scraps for butterflies

3¾ yds. peach solid for blocks, borders, and binding

2¾ yds. muslin for border and block backgrounds

5½ yds. backing fabric

Cutting

From the assorted scraps, cut:

30 butterflies, using the template on page 90.

From the peach, cut:

20 squares, each 9½" x 9½", for blocks

5 squares, each 14" x 14", for side setting triangles

2 squares, each 7¼" x 7¼"; cut once diagonally to yield 4 corner setting triangles

2 strips, each 5" x 68½", for outer border

2 strips, each 5" x 91", for outer border

From the muslin, cut:

30 squares, each 9½" x 9½", for block backgrounds

2 strips, each 2½" x 64½", for inner borders

2 strips, each 2½" x 81", for inner borders

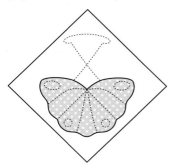

Butterfly Block

1. Position butterflies diagonally on the 30 background squares, and appliqué them in place.
2. Mark embroidery lines on the butterfly and background. Embroider wing lines on the butterflies and antennae on the blocks.

Quilt Top Assembly

1. Referring to the quilt plan, above left, arrange Butterfly blocks, alternate blocks and setting triangles in a diagonal setting. Sew the blocks together in rows. (See "Diagonal Settings" on page 15.)
2. Using the peach and muslin border strips, apply a mitered border. (See "Borders with Mitered Corners" on pages 65–66.)

Finishing

Refer to "Finishing Vintage Quilts" on pages 65–74.

1. Press the finished quilt top and mark the quilting design.
2. Layer the quilt top with batting and backing. Baste and quilt.
3. Bind the edges.
4. Sign and date your Butterfly quilt.

Dresden Plate

Another treasure Joyce Braus found in her mother's cedar chest was a set of twelve Dresden Plate blocks made by her grandmother, Anna Michulka. "I didn't know they existed. A Grandmother's Flower Garden quilt top was hidden away too," Joyce said. "The quilts bring much joy to my life, just knowing they are a part of my heritage. I was pleased to find someone to finish the quilts because I discovered after one quilting class, that I, like my mother, am not a quilter."

Dresden Plate *blocks circa 1930, by Anna Michulka, Eagle, Texas, 78" x 98". A double border enhances this traditional lattice setting. Completed by The Quilt Shop, 1989.*

Quilt size: 78" x 98"
Block size: 16½" x 16½"
Number of blocks: 12
Setting: Side by side with lattice

Materials

4 yds. blue solid for lattice, outer border, and binding

5¾ yds. muslin for blocks and inner borders

3 yds. (total) assorted medium and light print scraps for plate wedges (or 12 vintage Dresden Plates.)

6 yds. muslin for backing

Cutting

From the blue solid, cut:

8 strips, each 4" x 17", for lattice

5 strips, each 4" x 57", for lattice and inner border

2 strips, each 4" x 84", for lattice

2 strips, each 5" x 68", for outer top and bottom border

2 strips, each 5" x 98", for outer side borders

From the muslin, cut:

2 strips, each 2½" x 64", for inner top and bottom borders

2 strips, each 2½" x 88", for inner side borders

12 squares, 17" x 17", for block backgrounds

From the assorted scraps, cut:

216 Dresden plate wedges, using the template on page 91. Allow a ¼"-wide seam allowance around each template.

Block Assembly

Join plate wedges to make Dresden Plate circles or use vintage Dresden Plate circles. Appliqué the circles to background squares of muslin, and finish the center circle edges. (See "Appliquéing Dresden Plate Units" on opposite page.)

Quilt Top Assembly

1. Join 4 rows of 3 blocks each, adding 4" x 17" lattice strips between them.

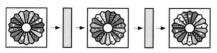

Make 4 rows.

2. Mark the 4" x 57" lattice strips. See "Straight Lattice Settings" on page 17. Sew the strips between the rows of blocks, matching the marks to the seam lines of the short lattice strips.

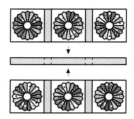

3. Measure and add lattice strips to the top and bottom of the quilt top, then to the sides. Miter the corners.

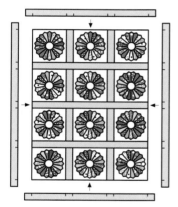

4. Measure the length and width of the quilt top through the center. Mark as required for mitered borders.

5. Join the middle and outer borders, matching centers, before applying to the quilt as a single unit. Miter the corners.

Finishing

Refer to "Finishing Vintage Quilts" on pages 65–74.

1. Press the finished quilt top and mark the quilting design.

2. Layer the quilt top with batting and backing. Baste and quilt.

3. Bind the edges.

4. Sign and date your Dresden Plate quilt.

Appliquéing Dresden Plate Units

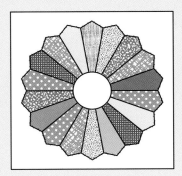

Dresden Plate Block

You may have completed Dresden Plate units, or perhaps unfinished wedges. The first step in making a Dresden Plate quilt is to join the wedges that make up the plate. There are two common types—those with pointed wedges and those with curved wedges.

I use two different methods to prepare Dresden Plate units for appliqué.

Pressing-Guide Method
1. Trace a single finished wedge onto an index card to use as a pressing guide.
2. Wash the pieces. While pressing them dry, use the guide and move the iron carefully around the edge, creasing the seam line so that it will turn under smoothly.

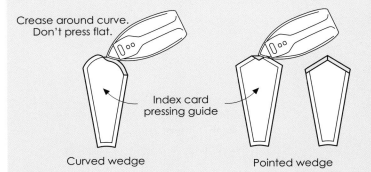

Crease around curve.
Don't press flat.

Index card
pressing guide

Curved wedge   Pointed wedge

Freezer-Paper Method
1. Cut a freezer-paper piece in the finished size and shape of the plate wedge.
2. Place the freezer-paper shape on a wedge, ¼" from the curved edge. Press it in place on the wrong side of a wedge, coated side down. The edge of the freezer paper is your stitching guide. When you appliqué, turn under the seam allowance with the tip of your needle. When the appliqué is complete, reach through the center opening to remove the freezer paper.

Freezer paper

NOTE

If your wedges have been stitched all the way to the edge of the fabric, you may need to remove a few stitches to free the seam allowance. Turn the seam allowance under and appliqué the wedges to the background.

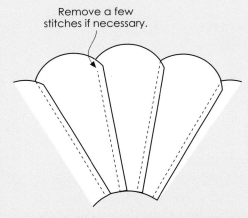

Remove a few
stitches if necessary.

Assembly

1. Center the plate unit on the background fabric and appliqué in place. Add a decorative buttonhole stitch with embroidery floss.
2. To make the quilting easier, cut away the background fabric under the appliqué. This allows the appliqué to lie flat over the batting in the finished quilt.

NOTE

Floss is the weakest thread in common use. Many old appliqué quilts show evidence of this where pieces appliquéd with floss are no longer attached, so appliqué with sewing thread and embellish with embroidery, using floss.

(continued on next page)

If the inner edge on the old plates appears even and sturdy, turn it under and stitch it to the background. Finish an uneven center with a circle of background or contrast fabric appliquéd over the edges. Examples of both techniques are plentiful in vintage quilts.

To make a perfect circle for the center of a Dresden Plate, use a compass to draw a circle on freezer paper. Make it large enough to cover the center opening; add a ¼"-wide seam allowance. Cut one freezer-paper circle for each plate

Cut ¼" away from freezer paper.

unit. Press the coated side of the paper to the wrong side of the center fabric. Cut out the fabric circles, leaving a ¼"-wide seam allowance around the freezer paper circles.

Position the circle over the center of the plate unit and pin. Using a thread to match the circle, needle-turn the edge and stitch in place.

Turn the finished block over and snip the background fabric away, leaving a ¼"-wide seam allowance. Remove the freezer paper.

Embroidered Collage

I arranged sixteen embroidered pieces, sized with a variety of framing techniques, in the manner of a photo montage. These blocks are characteristic of ones often found, slightly fragrant from sachet, in a chest of drawers at an estate sale. Although this setting would not have been used in the 1930s, the look of the quilt is reminiscent of that era. Reduce or enlarge this arrangement to accommodate any block style.

Embroidered Collage, *Sharon L. Newman, 1993, Lubbock, Texas, 36" x 47½". This sampler shows a variety of embroidery and framing styles.*

Quilt size: 36" x 47½"
Block size: 10" x 10"
Number of blocks: 12
Setting: Side by side with lattice

Materials

3¼ yds. green solid for borders, backing, and binding

3 yds. (total) of ¼-yd. pieces of assorted multicolored prints

Assorted embroidered linen pieces

Cutting

From the green solid, cut:

8 strips, each 2" x 10½", for short lattice

5 strips, each 2" x 33½", for horizontal lattice and top and bottom borders

2 strips, each 2" x 48", for side borders

Quilt Top Assembly

1. Create 12 blocks, each 10½" x 10½," by framing the linen pieces as desired with the multi-colored prints.

2. Plan an arrangement for the blocks.

3. Make 4 rows of 3 blocks each, adding 2" x 10½" lattice strips between the blocks.

Make 4 rows of blocks and lattice.

4. Mark and sew the 2" x 33½" lattice strips between the rows, matching the marks between the blocks on the long lattice to the seam lines of the short lattice. (See "Straight Lattice Settings" on page 17.)

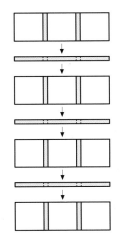

Embroidered Collage Framing Styles

A. Cameo
B. Butted frame
C. Attic Window
D. Mitered frame
E. Split color frame
F. Log Cabin
G. Partial block
H. Grouping

5. Stitch 2" x 33½" border strips to the top and bottom edges of the quilt top. Add the remaining 2" x 48" side borders.

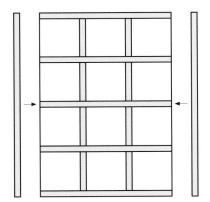

Finishing

Refer to "Finishing Vintage Quilts" on pages 65–74.

1. Press the finished quilt top and mark the quilting design.

2. Layer the quilt top with batting and backing. Baste and quilt.

3. Bind the edges.

4. Sign and date your quilt.

Double Pinwheel

Charlotte and Harold Simms brought a large box full of unfinished quilt projects to The Quilt Shop. The patchwork blocks were made by the mothers and grandmothers of each of the Simms. These large triangles, string pieced during the 1940s by Harold's grandmother, Etna Adams Hunter, were left in the box each time a new project was chosen for completion, because a satisfactory setting design had not been found.

We found this Double Pinwheel design while searching a pattern encyclopedia. Mr. Simms approved the design and the selected fabric to complete his grandmother's quilt.

Many of the family quilts inherited by Charlotte and Harold Simms, as well as the projects completed from blocks in the box, now decorate the beds of Roseville Manor, the Simmses' bed-and-breakfast inn, in Jefferson, Texas.

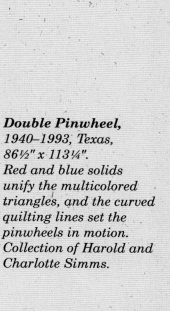

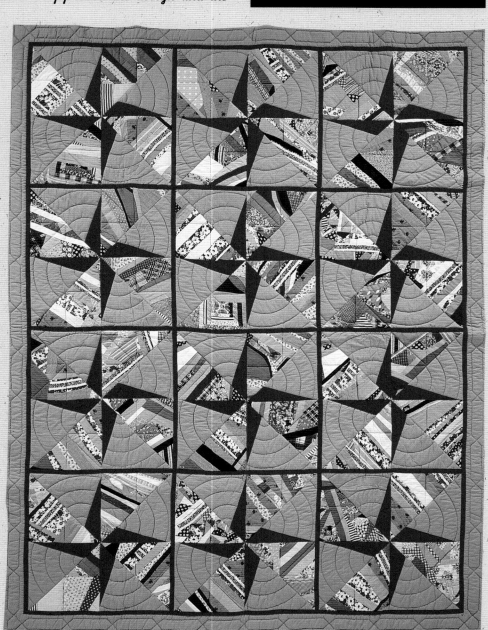

Double Pinwheel,
1940–1993, Texas,
86½" x 113¼".
Red and blue solids unify the multicolored triangles, and the curved quilting lines set the pinwheels in motion.
Collection of Harold and Charlotte Simms.

Quilt size: 86½" x 113¼"
Block size: 26" x 26"
Number of blocks: 12
Setting: Straight with lattice

Materials

12 yds. Williamsburg blue solid for blocks,
    outer border, and backing
3 yds. holly berry red solid for blocks and lattice
48 string-pieced triangles, cut from Template A

Cutting

(See "Making Templates" above right.)
From the blue, cut:
48 Template B
 2 strips, each 3" x 81½", for outer borders
 2 strips, each 3" x 114", for outer borders

From the red, cut:
48 Template C
 8 strips, each 1¼" x 27", for lattice
 5 strips, each 1¼" x 80", for lattice.
    Cut strips from the length of the fabric.
 2 strips, each 1¼" x 108½", for lattice.
    Cut strips from the length of the fabric.

Making Templates

1. Draw a 13½" square on graph paper. Draw a line from corner to corner.
2. To create the small pinwheel template, measure 4½" from one corner along the diagonal line. Connect that point to the adjacent corner. Trace each of the 3 shapes onto template material and label as shown. Add ¼"-wide seam allowances when cutting.

Block Assembly

1. Use Template A to cut triangles from pieces of vintage string-piecing. Or if necessary, string piece 48 new triangles, using Template A to ensure even sizing.
2. Sew each red triangle to a blue triangle. Sew the red/blue triangle units to the string-pieced triangles to make 48 squares.

Make 48.

3. Join four blocks, rotating the blocks to form the large pinwheel pattern. Make 12 Pinwheel blocks.

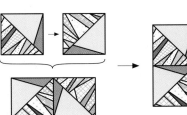

Quilt Top Assembly

Refer to "Straight Lattice Settings" on page 17.

1. Join Pinwheel blocks and 1¼" x 27" lattice strips to form 4 rows of 3 blocks each.
2. Mark the 1¼" x 80" lattice strips. Join the lattice strips and rows of blocks. Add one lattice strip each to the top and bottom of the quilt top.

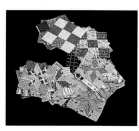

3. Mark the 1¼" x 108½" lattice strips and sew them to the sides, matching marks to blocks and horizontal lattice strips.

Finishing

Refer to "Finishing Vintage Quilts" on pages 65–74.

1. Press the finished quilt top and mark the quilting design.
2. Layer the quilt top with batting and backing. Baste and quilt.
3. Bind the edges.
4. Sign and date your Double Pinwheel quilt.

Stars and Ninepatches

The wait was worth it! Ten years after I acquired these blocks at an estate sale in 1982, reproduction fabrics became available with the appropriate colors and prints to finish the quilt. The brown fabrics in the blocks were produced in the 1860s, while the rich copper colors are excellent examples of the madder prints of 1875.

Dry goods stores stocked small prints in tone-on-tone pink from the 1860s through the 1920s. (Note the star with double pink-print diamonds in the photograph.) The fabric in the yellow-green star is characteristic of greens from the 1840s. The contemporary dark blue-green lattice fabric resembles the typical green of the 1860s. Unfortunately, the green dyes of old were often fugitive; they faded, leaving only tan.

Piping detail from Stars and Nine-patches border.

Stars and Nine Patches, Sharon L. Newman, 1993, Lubbock, Texas, 87" x 116". Madder print blocks take on an even richer, more elegant appearance in the finished quilt.

No two of these thirty-five blocks were the same size, with the Ninepatch blocks as much as ¾" larger than the Star blocks. I sized the blocks using the straight framing method described on pages 8–9. Two of the Ninepatch blocks were in poor condition, so I repaired them with appropriate reproduction fabrics.

The number of Star and Ninepatch blocks prevented me from alternating the patterns exactly, thus inspiring the final symmetrical, but unusual, arrangement. The setting uses all the blocks and a wide lattice to create a finished quilt that is 98" x 116". The width of the lattice and the finished quilt size are consistent with quilt styles of the third quarter of the nineteenth century.

To duplicate this quilt, you need fifteen Ninepatch blocks and twenty Star blocks of the desired size.

Common quilting patterns found on the wide lattices in old quilts include grids, orange peel, and pumpkin seeds. In this quilt, the lattices are quilted with an elongated orange-peel shape with a pumpkin-seed center. Quilting outlines the Star blocks, and a cross-and-box quilting design overlays the Ninepatches. The outer border is quilted in angled, parallel straight lines. See full size orange peel quilting design on page 92.

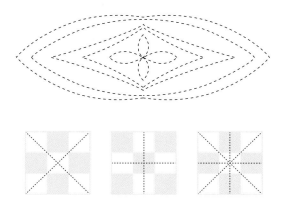

I inserted piping in the binding. This technique is sometimes seen on quilts from the 1870s, but more often on quilts from earlier decades. See photograph on page 48.

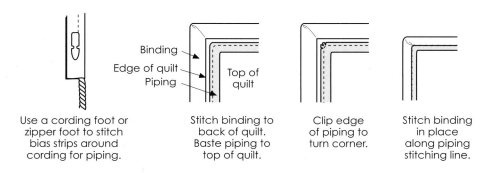

Use a cording foot or zipper foot to stitch bias strips around cording for piping.

Stitch binding to back of quilt. Baste piping to top of quilt.

Clip edge of piping to turn corner.

Stitch binding in place along piping stitching line.

Madder Prints

Madder was the most commonly used dye of the eighteenth- and nineteenth- century textile industry. The vegetable dye used for red, rust, copper, and orange prints of the period came from the root of the madder plant. The hue these dyes produced depended on the mordant, or chemical, used to fix the dye. After 1869, dyeing with madder root decreased as the textile industry discovered synthetic compounds for dyeing "madder" colors.[7]

Vintage Recipe for Home Dyeing with Madder Red

To each pound of goods, alum, 5 ounces; red, or cream tartar, 1 ounce. Put in the goods and bring the kettle to a boil, for one-half hour; then air them and boil one-half hour longer; empty the kettle and fill with clean water; put in bran, 1 peck, make it milk warm, and let it stand until the bran rises; then skim off the bran and put in one-half pound madder; put in the goods and heat slowly until it boils and is done. Wash in strong suds.[8]

1898 Stars in Garden Maze

In the summer of 1979, three members of a family entered The Quilt Shop burdened with boxes and sacks of unfinished quilt blocks. They sought names for the different block patterns and guidance as to the complexity of the work needed to make the pieces into quilts.

The family spread out eleven projects for discussion. Jacob's Ladder blocks and Grandmother's Fan blocks were complete and ready for setting. Some seamstress had joined squares of string-pieced scraps into a few bigger blocks, and these string-pieced stars were stacked in a white box with a gold lid. Believing all of the projects were from the 1930s, the family was surprised to learn that the stars probably were made much earlier.

After discussing the projects with us, the trio gathered all the projects back into the containers and

1898 Stars in Garden Maze, *Sharon L. Newman, 1993, Lubbock, Texas, 95" x 95". Vintage fabrics complete string-pieced stars in a very graphic setting.*

left to contact other family members about finishing the quilts. Family members adopted the most complete of the 1930s projects and returned and sold the remainder to The Quilt Shop.

When I examined the string-pieced stars more closely than before, I found an 1898 date on the newspaper foundation. There were twenty-three stars. When my mother-in-law, Bessie Newman, saw the black and red prints, she retrieved a metal can from the barn. Similar print strings saved from her mother's scraps filled the can. We selected enough pieces to sew another star to even the number to 24, making a 4 x 6 block setting possible.

Over the next fourteen years, I purchased vintage fabrics for the star "fill-ins," the lattice, and the border.

The condition of the stars led to a diagonal setting, which allowed damaged blocks to be used at the half-square triangle positions where only the best parts were needed. The Garden Maze setting is a dramatic frame for the bold star colors. A variety of black-on-white shirting prints form the star backgrounds. The sashing is a turn-of-the-century black-on-red print only 24" wide. The vintage stripe used in the lattice was 33" wide. Careful calculations ensured that enough vintage fabric was available to complete the project. Creating a quilt from limited resources is part of the challenge and pleasure of working with vintage pieces.

Quilt size: 90" x 90"
Block size: 14½" x 14½"
Number of blocks: 13 whole blocks, 8 half-blocks, and 4 quarter blocks
Setting: Diagonal with lattice

Materials

5 yds. red 24"-wide vintage fabric or
    3 yds. 45"-wide contemporary fabric
3 yds. white 33"-wide vintage fabric or
    2¾ yds. 45"-wide contemporary fabric
4½ yds. vintage background prints
If you do not have vintage blocks, add 4 yds.
    assorted scraps of print fabrics for
    string-pieced stars.
Lightweight cardboard for pressing template

Cutting

From the red, cut:
    4   strips, each 1½" x 84½", for inner borders
    4   strips, each 1½" x 91½", for outer borders
    34 strips, each 1½" x 15½", for frames
    38 strips, each 1½" x 16½", for frames
    36 strips, each 1½" x 4¾", for Xs

From the white, cut:
    4   strips, each 2¾" x 89½", for middle border
    2   strips, each 2¾" x 22½", for lattice
    2   strips, each 2¾" x 60½", for lattice
    2   strips, each 2¾" x 100½", for lattice
    18 strips, each 2¾" x 16½", for lattice

From the background prints, cut:
    84 corner squares, using Template A on page 92
    72 side triangles, using Template B on page 91
    72 strips, each 1" x 15", for framing vintage
        stars, if needed

Block Assembly

1. If you wish to piece stars for this quilt, use Template C on page 91. Make the required number of whole and partial blocks.

Half-Star
Make 8.

Quarter-Star
Make 4.

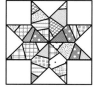
Star Block
Make 13.

2. If you have unfinished, vintage Star blocks, measure the star points for the corner squares and side triangles. (See pages 32–33 for instructions on adding squares and triangles to Star blocks.) If necessary, sew 1"-wide strips of background fabric to the edges of the Star blocks to bring them all to the same size. (See instructions for this technique on page 33.) The vintage blocks were cut 15" x 15" to finish as 14½" squares.

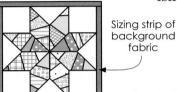

Sizing strip of background fabric

3. Sew red lattice strips to two sides of each block, then to the other two sides.

Quilt Top Assembly

1. Arrange the blocks in a diagonal setting with 2¾" x 16½" white lattice strips between them. Sew the blocks and lattice strips together in diagonal rows.
2. Mark the long lattice strips for placement and join them to the rows of blocks as for a straight setting with lattice. (See page 17.)

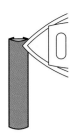

3. Cut a 1" x 4¾" piece of lightweight cardboard to use as a pressing template. Fold the 1½" x 4¾" red strips over it and press.

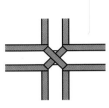

4. Position the pressed strips in an X on the long lattice strips so that they "connect" the corners of the Star blocks. Appliqué the strips in place, turning the ends under.

5. Press and trim the quilt top. Mark and sew the top and bottom 1½" x 84½" red border strips to the quilt top. Then add the inner side borders.
6. Measure, mark, and sew the 2¾" x 89½" white strips to the top and bottom of the quilt, then to the sides.
7. Add the 1½" x 84½" red outer border strips in the same way.

Finishing

Refer to "Finishing Vintage Quilts" on pages 65–74.
1. Press the finished quilt top and mark the desired quilting design.
2. Layer the quilt top with batting and backing. Baste and quilt.

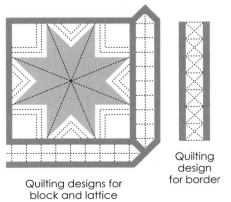

Quilting designs for block and lattice

Quilting design for border

3. Bind the edges.
4. Sign and date your Stars in Garden Maze quilt.

Fortune Cookie

Four Drunkard's Path blocks, made with string piecing in the curved section of the block, form each of the 10" compound blocks of the Medallion pattern. Nita Fry made the blocks in Hamlin, Texas, in 1935.

In 1992, Jane Hayes designed the medallion-like setting and completed the quilt. She quilted a bamboo design in the muslin border, a curved feather in the outer border, and a sampler of different small designs in the Marble blocks. The same little flower design appears in all of the intersecting corners. Straight diagonal lines of quilting fill the navy sashing.

Fortune Cookie, 1935–1992, Texas and New Mexico, 92" x 101". A Drunkard's Path unit was string pieced and set in a medallion variation. Pieced by Nita Fry Wright, quilted by Jane Haynes. Collection of Jackie Rayroux, niece of Nita Fry Wright.

Colonial Ladies

Ten ladies elegantly displayed in oval Cameo blocks frame a garden full of flowers. A blue print and a cream-and-blue background combine to shape the medallion-style arrangement.

The Cameo blocks echo the oval center panel of painted flowers. The flower colors repeat the colors of the ladies' dresses, which are neatly outlined with black running stitches.

This setting includes a pillow tuck so that all the pattern blocks show when the quilt is arranged on a bed. In the tradition of many old quilts, this one has borders only where necessary, on the sides and at the foot of the bed.

Colonial Ladies, 1930–1989, Texas, 80" x 100". This Cameo medallion setting uses the ten available blocks in a charming fashion. Collection of Mary Phy.

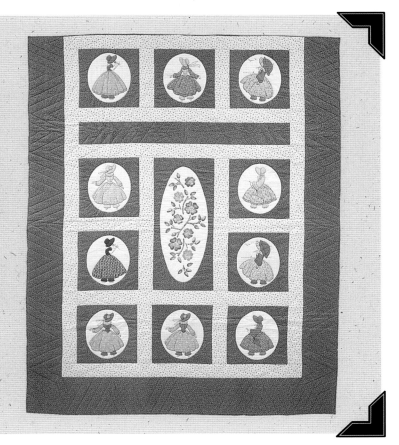

Quilt size: 82" x 103"
Block size: 16" x 16"
Number of blocks:
      10 plus center rectangle
Setting: Medallion

Materials

2¾ yds. light print for lattice
5 yds. blue print for block frames, borders,
    and binding
4 yds. 90"-wide muslin for block backgrounds
    and backing
10 Vintage Colonial Ladies blocks or scraps
    of assorted prints for Colonial Ladies
Fabric dye, embroidery floss, or fabric scraps
    to create the center panel flower design

Cutting

From the light print, cut:
  6 strips, each 4½" x 16½", for lattice
  2 strips, each 4½" x 36½", for lattice
  5 strips, each 4½" x 56½", for lattice
      Cut strips from the length of the fabric.
  2 strips, each 4½" x 94½", for lattice
      Cut strips from the length of the fabric.

From the blue print, cut:
 10 squares, each 16½" x 16½", for frames
  1 rectangle, 16½" x 36½", for frame

  1 strip, 6½" x 56½", for pillow tuck
  1 strip, 9½" x 64½", for top and bottom
      borders
  2 strips, each 9½" x 103½", for side borders

From the muslin, cut:
  1 rectangle, 16" x 34", for center panel
      background
 10 squares, each 16½" x 16½", for block
      backgrounds

Block Assembly

1. Using the squares of blue-print fabric, frame 10 vintage blocks in cameo fashion as shown on page 10. Or, using the templates on the pullout pattern at the back of the book, appliqué 10 Colonial Ladies blocks and frame them with the blue print fabric.

2. On the 16" x 34" muslin rectangle, paint flowers with fabric dye (or embroider or appliqué the flowers). Use the pullout pattern or make one of your own.

3. Using the 16½" x 36½" blue-print rectangle, frame the center oval panel. (See pages 10–11.) Cut this opening 13" wide and 32" long.

Quilt Top Assembly

See "Straight Lattice Settings" on page 17.

1. Use two 4½" x 16½" light print strips to join three Cameo blocks for the top row. Make a second set of three blocks with two lattice strips for the bottom row.

2. Sew a 4½" x 16½" light print strip between two blocks, in a vertical arrangement, for the side panels. Make two vertical rows.

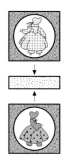

3. Mark 4½" x 36½" light-print strips and join the center oval with blocks on either side as shown.

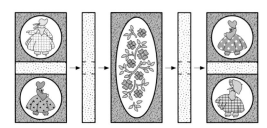

4. Assemble the quilt top as shown, being careful to mark the long lattice strips so you can match them to the lattice seam lines.

5. Add the 9½" x 64½" blue print strip to the bottom of the quilt top. Add one 9½" x 103½" blue print strip to each side.

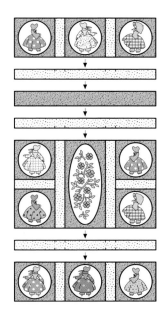

Finishing

Refer to "Finishing Vintage Quilts" on pages 65–74.

1. Press the finished quilt top and mark the quilting design. Outline the center flowers and ladies. Mark straight lines to form crisscross patterns in the lattice and draw a zigzag pattern along the outer borders.
2. Layer the quilt top with batting and backing. Baste and quilt.
3. Bind the edges.
4. Sign and date your Colonial Ladies quilt.

Changes in Fabric and Design

Wonderful new fabrics appeared on the market after World War I. Newly imported German dyes produced clear, bright colors. After the war, America produced "greige" goods of better quality, in greater supply, and fairly priced. "Easter egg" colors in pink, yellow, blue, green, and lavender characterized the fabrics of this period. In addition to the many solid colors, small prints were produced in coordinating colors.

Quiltmaking quickly assimilated changing design styles such as Art Nouveau and Art Deco.

Appliqué suited the curves, flowers, and vines of the Art Nouveau motifs. Pieced quilts more accurately adapted the angular, stylized designs of Art Deco.

In 1921 Marie Webster and two friends, Ida Hes and Evangeline Beshore, founded the Practical Patchwork Company, specializing in stamped or pre-cut quilt kits. Mail-order pattern companies and home-based quilt-kit production made new designs accessible to quiltmakers in all parts of the country.

Cameo Tulips

Jackie French brought the Tulip blocks to The Quilt Shop for consultation. The forty-five blocks presented quite a design challenge. Graceful tulips in clear, solid colors were hand-appliquéd to muslin backgrounds with matching embroidery floss in a close satin stitch.

The tulip design was a little large for the muslin background squares, and the quiltmaker had not always centered the tulip on the muslin square before stitching it in place. This Art Nouveau style setting maintains the graceful shapes of the Tulip blocks, while the oval cameo gives consistency to the design and construction.

Cameo Tulips, *blocks circa 1920, Texas, 96" x 111". This Art-Nouveau setting complements the flowers. Collection of Jackie French.*

Quilt size: 96" x 96"
Block size: 15" x 15"
Number of blocks: 36
Size of oval opening: 10½" x 12¾"
Setting: Side by side

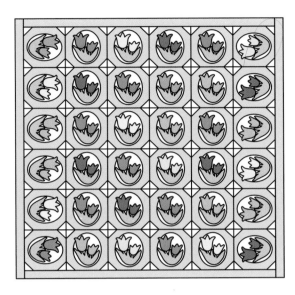

Materials

7½ yds. blue solid for block frames, borders and binding

1¼ yds. of 45"-wide muslin for corner triangles

3⅓ yds. of 108"-wide muslin for backing

Cutting

From the blue, cut:

36 squares, each 15½" x 15½", for frames

2 strips, each 3½" x 90½", for borders. Cut strips from the length of the fabric.

2 strips, each 3½" x 96½", for borders. Cut strips from the length of the fabric.

From the 45"-wide muslin, cut:

36 squares, each 6¼" x 6¼"; cut the squares twice diagonally to yield 144 triangles.

Block Assembly

1. Create 36 Cameo blocks using your vintage blocks and the 15½" squares of blue fabric. (See "Oval and Circular Frames" on pages 10–11.) If you wish to appliqué

the Tulip blocks pictured here, use the templates on pages 93–94.

2. Instead of piecing inset squares, which are more difficult, mark a point 3⅛" from each corner on each side of each Cameo block. Mark lines on the blocks from point to point as shown. Cut away the corners of the blocks.

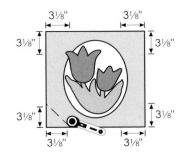

3. Sew a muslin triangle to each corner of each block. Press seams toward the center of the block.

Quilt Top Assembly

1. Arrange the blocks in the color sequence desired, using 6 rows of blocks across and 6 rows down.

2. Sew the blocks together in rows. Press seams of even-numbered rows in one direction, and odd-numbered rows in the other direction. Join the rows, matching the seam lines between the blocks and easing as necessary.

3. Sew the 3½" x 90½" blue strips to the top and bottom of the quilt top. Then add the 3½" x 96½" blue strips to the sides.

Finishing

Refer to "Finishing Vintage Quilts" on pages 65–74.

1. Press the finished quilt top and mark the quilting design. Outline the tulips and leaves, the oval openings around the flowers, and the corner squares. Draw 4" flowers in the connecting squares.

2. Layer the quilt top with batting and backing. Baste and quilt.

3. Bind the edges.

4. Sign and date your Cameo Tulips quilt.

Pattern Quilts

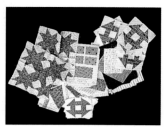

Before patterns were printed, quiltmakers often shared a design by giving a pieced block to a friend. Many quiltmakers kept a block of each design they pieced. Collections sometimes spanned several decades. The blocks were usually not the same size, nor sewn of the same fabrics. Some quiltmakers sewed all of their "pattern blocks" into a sampler style quilt as a "last" quilt.

I received some fabric "pattern blocks" in the 1960s. I was teaching in an Austin, Texas, high school. I stitched some quilt pieces during my lunch hours, and an elderly cleaning lady asked if I would like some of her patterns. She gave me a maple leaf appliquéd block, a block with a large strawberry, and a pieced Dresden Plate.

Pattern Quilt

Mary Ellen Copeland was born in Indiana in 1845. She married Henry H. Young in Independence, Arkansas, in 1862. He fought in the Civil War.

In 1870 they moved to Texas. In 1881, Mary Ellen had five small children when she was widowed at age 36. Three other children died in infancy, one of them eight days after Henry's death.

Pattern Quilt by Mary Ellen Copeland Young, 1895, Texas, 68" x 94". This legacy of designs, probably Mary Ellen's "pattern book," shows a bold use of color as the various sizes and patterns of the blocks come together in the medallion setting. Collection of Betty J. Mills.

Mary Ellen applied for a Civil War widow's pension and tenaciously wrote letters for ten years until she was granted the sum of $8.00 per month in 1891. She received an increase to $12.00 per month in 1908.

Betty Mills, great-granddaughter of the quiltmaker, related that "the females in my family have traditionally valued independence and creative expression."

This quilt is a legacy of designs, probably Mary Ellen's pattern book, executed in a single quilt. Thirty-eight blocks, of several patterns in different sizes, are joined with strips, forming a medallion-style quilt. The center medallion features a feathered-star motif. All of the blocks are pieced, and the only appliqués on the quilt are the four leaves in the corner squares of the center star.

The quilt includes typical fabrics from 1895: bold stripes, large windowpane checks, woven ginghams, florals, white stars on blue ground, blue chambray, black random dots on red, and several small allover designs in shades of pink. Navy and red colors dominate, but pink, blue, green, and black printed fabrics are used, with white shirting prints in tan, black, blue, and red. Quilting outlines the patchwork blocks, and straight quilting lines on a diagonal fill the border.

Pattern Quilt 1893–1993

Many pattern quilts jumble different-size blocks together randomly. Some pattern quilts have a medallion-style setting with a large block at the center. I arranged twenty-five vintage quilt block patterns in a strippy-style setting. This quilt is more orderly than some pattern quilts because all of the blocks were sized to fourteen inches.

The blocks contain prints and fabrics typical of the fourth quarter of the nineteenth century. The setting fabric is a maroon tone that was printed in many designs but available only briefly during the 1890s. The black and gray prints exhibit the variety of "Shaker" prints produced into the new century.

Following are the names of each of the twenty-five patterns, along with a brief description of the steps taken to prepare each vintage block for the quilt.

All the pattern names are from the *Encyclopedia of Pieced Quilt Patterns* compiled by Barbara Brackman, except the Chips and Whetstones, Dove in the Window, and Fish blocks, which I found in *Quiltmaker's Big Book of 14" Block Patterns* by C. Anthony and L. Lehman.

1. **Windmill**. Other names include: Mosaic, Water Wheel, Mill Wheel, Old Crow, Fly, Crow's Foot, Water Mill, Sugar Bowl, Kathy's Ramble, Fan Mill, and Pinwheel. I added triangles and a ½"-wide frame.

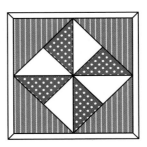

Windmill

Pattern Quilt 1893–1993

Pattern Quilt *1893–1993, Sharon L. Newman, 1993, Lubbock, Texas, 82" x 92". Vintage blocks, vintage fabrics, and traditional patterns in a strippy sampler setting.*

2. Yankee Puzzle. I framed this block with 1½"-wide dark print strips and 1¼"-wide light print strips.

Yankee Puzzle

3. Dove in the Window. Other names include: Four Swallows, Airplanes, and Blue Birds for Happiness. I redrafted the templates and recut and pieced the star shape. I filled in light-print triangles and light/dark pieced corner squares.

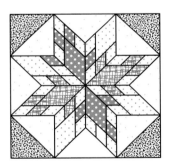

Dove in the Window

4. At the Square. Other names include: Fireside Visitor, Rope and Anchor, Arrow, and Colorado's Arrowhead. I added a 1¾"-wide frame.

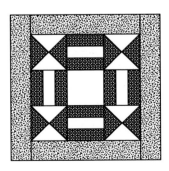

At the Square

5. Shoo Fly. Other names include: Sherman's March, Love Knot, Hole in the Barn Door, Monkey Wrench, and Quail's Nest. I grouped four vintage blocks to make one large block.

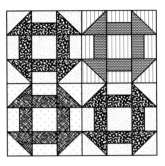

Shoo Fly

6. Domino Net. I pieced this block from vintage fabrics after drafting a 14" square pattern.

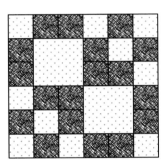

Domino Net

7. North Wind. I added triangles to each edge of the block and framed it with strips.

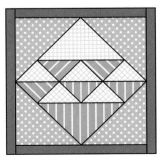

North Wind

8. King's Crown. I added triangles to each edge of the block and 2"-wide framing strips.

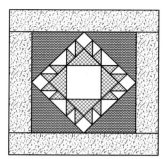

King's Crown

9. Cake Stand. I added triangles to each edge of the block and framed it with 1⅝"-wide strips of light print.

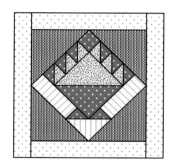

Cake Stand

10. Devil's Claws. I marked the seam allowance with a template for a 14" finished block. There are two Devil's Claws blocks in this quilt.

Devil's Claws

11. Mystic Maze. Other names include: Denver, Boston Pavement, Spider Web, Merry Go Round, Amazing Windmill, and Autumn Leaves. I added a ⅞"-wide dark print frame and a 1⅜"-wide medium print frame.

Mystic Maze

12. Morning Star. Other names include Rosebud and Virginia. I added 1¼"-wide light print strips to each side of the block, then added 1"-wide dark print strips and filled the corners with squares of the same dark print.

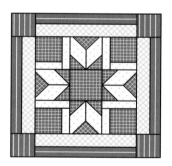

Morning Star

13. Chips and Whetstones. I cut and pieced vintage fabrics for this block.

Chips and Whetstones

14. *Ninepatch Variation.* I added a 2⅓"-wide frame.

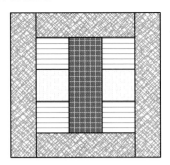

Ninepatch Variation

15. *Evening Star.* I added background fabric and double framing with patchwork corners.

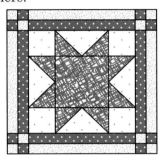

Evening Star

16. *Pattern Unknown.* I added triangles to each block edge.

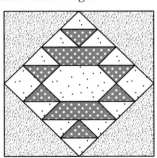

Pattern Unknown

17. *Ninepatch Star.* I drafted a 14" square block and used the original block at center, coordinating it with vintage fabrics.

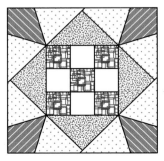

Ninepatch Star

18. *Double X.* Other names include: Fox and Geese and Crosses and Losses. I added ¾"-wide and 1¼"-wide frames.

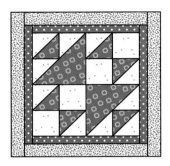

Double X

19. *Flutter Wheel Variation.* The pieced border was part of the original block. The uneven measure of the block was disguised by the framing.

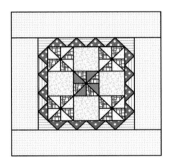

Flutter Wheel Variation

20. *Federal Chain.* Other names include: Flagstones, New Snowball, Improved Ninepatch, Snowball, Delaware's Flagstones, Aunt Patty's Favorite, Aunt Patsy's Pet, Four and Ninepatch, Dutch Mill, and Pullman Puzzle. I grouped four small blocks to make one larger block.

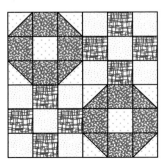

Federal Chain

21. Box Quilt. I framed this block with a ½"-wide dark print strip and a 1½"-wide light print strip.

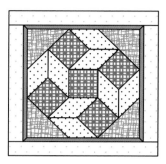

Box Quilt

23. Flying Geese. I pieced this block using vintage fabrics in colors to coordinate with the other blocks.

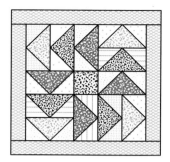

Flying Geese

22. Wheel of Chance. I appliquéd the vintage piece to a background and added corner triangles of a contrasting print.

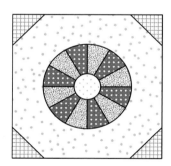

Wheel of Chance

24. Fish. I pieced this block using vintage fabrics.

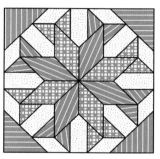

Fish

Quilt Pattern Names

A Boston rocker, according to quilt expert Ruth E. Finley, is recognized as such wherever it turns up. But the same is not true of quilt patterns. The earliest designs for quilts rarely had formal names the way they do now. Generic names like "hexagon patchwork" or "stencil quilt" could describe several arrangements of the particular units in one quilt.

As block quilts became more popular and the same patchwork combinations were made over and over again, quiltmakers began to name them.

Some names describe the design, while others seem quite fanciful.

In 1898, the Ladies Art Company recorded many of these designs, but they gave the blocks numbers instead of names. The first quilt history books listed block names, but did not always give sketches of the patterns.

Comprehensive lists of quilt pattern names, with sketches of the designs, exist today. Especially helpful are Barbara Brackman's *Encyclopedia of Pieced Quilt Patterns* and Judy Rehmel's *The Quilt I. D. Book.*

Finishing Vintage Quilts

Adding Borders

A well-planned border unifies the design and completes the quilt top. Study the types of borders used in the period when your vintage blocks were pieced (See the timeline on pages 12–14.)

Before adding borders, measure the quilt top. Press the quilt top, then fold it in half lengthwise to see if the side measurements are the same. Fold the bottom of the quilt up to the top to see if the widths match. Minor differences can be eased in sewing, but if the difference is an inch or more, make small adjustments in the seams of the quilt top to make the measurements the same.

Borders with Straight-Cut Corners

1. Measure the width of the quilt top through the center; cut 2 border strips to match this measurement.
2. Mark the centers of the top and bottom quilt edges with pins. Fold and mark again in fourths, then eighths. Fold and mark the centers of the border strips in the same fashion.

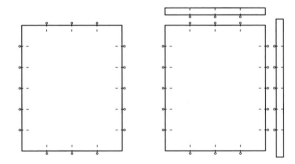

3. Match the pins as you pin the top and bottom borders to the quilt top. As you stitch each border, add more pins between the divisions as necessary to ensure that no stretching takes place.
4. To add the side borders, measure the length of the quilt top through the center again, including the top and bottom borders. Cut border strips to this measurement. Mark and sew as for top and bottom borders.

Borders with Mitered Corners

1. Measure the length and width of the quilt top through the center. Add two finished border widths to each measurement plus 2"–3" for seam allowances and a little extra mitering length. Cut border strips to match these measurements.
2. Mark the quilt top and borders as in step 2 at left for straight-cut borders. On the quilt top, mark ¼" from the edge of each corner. On the border strips, measure and mark half the length of the quilt top in each direction from the center pin.

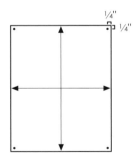

Measure through the center.
Mark corner seam intersections.

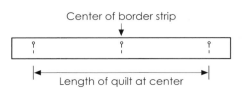

Center of border strip

Length of quilt at center

3. Pin each border strip to the quilt top, matching pins. The raw edges of the quilt top should match the outermost pin in the border strip. Sew the four borders to the quilt top; match pins and take care to start and end your stitching ¼" from the corners of the quilt top. Backstitch at each starting and stopping point.

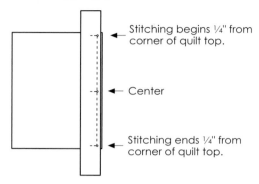

Stitching begins ¼" from corner of quilt top.

Center

Stitching ends ¼" from corner of quilt top.

4. Place one corner of the quilt on your work surface, right side up. Turn under a border strip at a 45° angle. Check the angle of the miter with a ruler for accuracy. Also check to make sure that the outer corner is square. Press and pin in place.

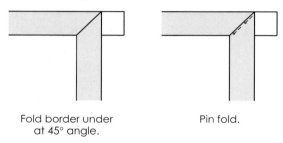

Fold border under at 45° angle.   Pin fold.

5. Fold the quilt, right sides together, matching the edges of the borders exactly. Stitch on the creased miter line from the inner border seam to the outer edge of the border.

6. Trim excess fabric, leaving a ¼"-wide seam allowance. Press the seam open.

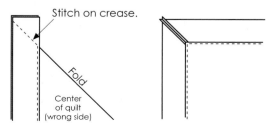

Stitch on crease.

Fold

Center of quilt (wrong side)

7. Repeat steps 4–6 with the remaining corners.

Planning Quilting Designs

Unfinished vintage quilt tops really change character with the addition of quilting lines. Some "busy" scrap quilts look best quilted all over with the old-fashioned shell design. More formal quilt designs look best with feathers, wreaths, or hearts in blocks, and cables, "pumpkin seeds," or grids in borders and backgrounds.

The quilting design is an important component of any quilt. The multitude of little stitches have two purposes. One is to connect the top, batting, and backing with sufficient stitching to keep the batting in place. Antique quilts with cotton batting were quilted with lines of stitching close together to maintain the evenness of the cotton bat. Modern polyester and cotton battings are more stable and allow quilters to leave more space between stitching lines. Most modern battings can safely be quilted with lines about two inches apart.

The second purpose of the quilting is to provide a part of the overall quilt design. The quilting design should enhance the quilt pattern, attach the three layers of the quilt evenly, and be enjoyable to stitch.

After you complete the patchwork or appliqué and attach the borders, press the entire quilt top in preparation for the next step: marking the quilting designs.

The quilting design can be plain or fancy. Simple outline quilting and "by-the-piece" (¼" away from the edges of all the pieces) quilting are traditional for certain quilt styles. Other quilts depend on fancy quilting with feathers, wreaths, or baskets. Many quilts have a combination of these in the final design.

For a quilt top made from vintage blocks, try to choose a quilting design appropriate to the period in which the blocks originated. Refer to the timeline on pages 12–14 for quilting styles suitable for various periods. Also consider the vintage fabrics when planning the quilting design.

Simple in-the-ditch (in the seam line) outline quilting may be adequate for weaker vintage fabrics.

In her book *Old Patchwork Quilts and the Women Who Made Them*, Ruth Finley listed the "commonest" quilting designs from old patchwork quilts: Horizontal, Crossbar, Double Crossbar, Diagonal, Diamond, Double Diamond, and Splint. "All these seven kinds of quilting were known as 'plain' because their lines were straight. Of 'fancy' quilting there were two types: 'block' and 'running' designs."[9] Many of the designs Finley listed relate to patchwork designs, for example, Spider Web, Dove of Peace, Star and Crown, Oak Leaf, and Wheel of Fortune. Feather wreaths, clamshells, and the familiar fan appeared as well. Her list of running designs includes vines, feathers, rope, chains, and "tea-cup." She explains that some of the designs were found in furniture and architecture.

Close observation of quilting patterns on old quilts provides clues for quilting vintage pieces. Study the quilts in calendars and state quilt documentation books. Find pictures of similar patterns. A magnifying lens often helps to reveal the quilting designs.

Quilting Designs

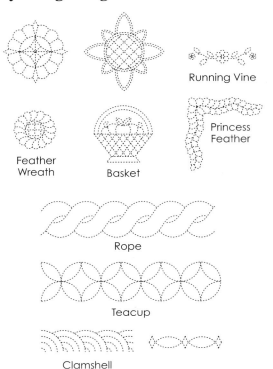

Running Vine

Feather Wreath

Basket

Princess Feather

Rope

Teacup

Clamshell

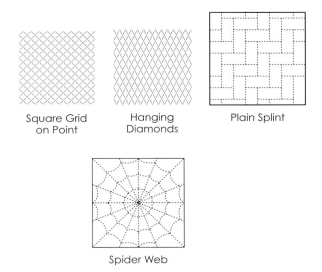

Square Grid on Point

Hanging Diamonds

Plain Splint

Spider Web

Marking Quilting Designs

You can quilt "by the piece," with no marking, by following the seam allowances with your needle by touch. Outline quilting in-the-ditch follows seam lines and does not require marking. Mark designs for blocks and borders with chalk or a silver marking pencil. Test the pencil on scraps of the fabrics to be marked. Vintage fabrics may not release markers as well as contemporary fabrics do. Use a gentle touch when marking, and if the pencil does not erase as you quilt, try brushing the line with a scrap of polyester batting. Exact replication of some old quilts requires the graphite pencil marks to remain, but the best-looking quilts show no marks.

Choosing Batting

There are many different battings suitable for use with vintage quilt tops. The batting you choose depends on the look you want to achieve and the type of quilting you want to do.

Cotton battings are common in vintage quilts. Cotton-polyester blends and 100% cotton are gentle on vintage fabrics, yielding a quilt with the feel of an antique.

Flannel was also used in old quilts. It produces a flat top but is difficult to hand quilt. Prewashing is essential for flannel as it shrinks considerably.

You may also choose a thin polyester batting for vintage quilt tops. The finished quilt will have the flatness of an old quilt even though quilting lines need not be spaced as close as with cotton batting. This is a real benefit for more fragile vintage fabrics.

A regular-weight polyester batting makes a fluffier quilt with higher loft. This may be an appropriate choice for poorly pieced tops that required considerable easing as pieces were sewn together and now have a good bit of fullness to quilt out.

Mountain Mist, a Legend in Batting

Mountain Mist has provided filling for quilts since 1846 when, in response to requests by their wives, George S. Stearns and Seth C. Foster combined forces to create a cotton batting that would not stretch or tear.

Their early "cotton wadding" was more compressed than hand-carded batting. It was the formula of paste made from flour and water applied to the cotton and dried on a marble slab that eventually satisfied the wives and their quilting friends. Thus, the partnership of Stearns and Foster began. They provided a source from which quilters could purchase smooth, even, cotton batting instead of laboriously hand carding small pieces of cotton to accumulate enough to fit a quilt top.

A company well known for mattresses and quilting supplies, Stearns and Foster has seen the United States through seven wars. The "cotton wadding" provided to the medical divisions and the cotton mattresses provided to the army and navy were made into batting during peacetime. The worst threat to business was the Civil War, when cotton was at issue in the conflict.

A 1933 advertisement describes "cotton already spread for you in one piece, bedspread size, 81 x 96 inches. Because of the exclusive Glazene, it may be handled like a piece of flannel. The fine, lacy web of the Glazene eliminates resistance to the quilter's needle. Uniform in thickness. No lint."

The company was also a leader in the development of polyester batting, with sales of this product beginning in the early 1960s.

Layering the Quilt Top, Batting, and Backing

1. Press the finished quilt top after the final border is added. Check the wrong side and re-press any seam allowances that were pressed incorrectly.

2. Measure the width and length of the quilt through the center. Cut and assemble the backing so that it extends two inches beyond the quilt top on all sides. Press seams open. (See the "Quilt Backings" yardage chart on page 75 for methods of seaming fabric lengths together for backings of the correct size.)

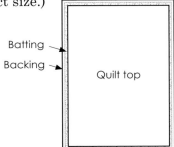

3. Check the batting package. Some cotton-blend bats require prewashing, and some polyester bats should be tumbled in a warm dryer to remove the fold lines.

4. Place the backing, wrong side up, on a large table or clean carpet. Spread the batting over the backing and trim the batting to match the backing. Center the quilt top on the batting and backing. Starting at the center of the quilt, pin all three layers together with 1" safety pins. Working out from the center, pin about every 8".

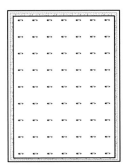

⊠ ⊠ ⊠ ⊠ ⊠ ⊠ ⊠ ⊠ ⊠ **NOTE** ⊠ ⊠ ⊠ ⊠ ⊠ ⊠ ⊠ ⊠ ⊠

Fold the backing over the batting and pin to "seal" the edges.

⊠ ⊠

Begin quilting in the center of the quilt. Continue to enlarge the quilted area from the center out. Work to make your stitches even, not just small.

Choosing Quilting Thread

Use cotton thread to quilt vintage fabrics. Do not use vintage thread, however, as the strength is not trustworthy. Do not use polyester thread, which is too strong for vintage fabrics.

When quilting vintage tops or blocks, it is appropriate to choose colored threads, instead of just white or ecru. Many vintage quilts show colored thread in the stitches on the backing. The Stars and Ninepatches Quilt on page 48 was quilted with red, green, and ecru threads.

The familiar cotton thread labeled "O.N.T." was developed in the 1860s by the Clark company for use with the new machines for sewing, as well as for hand sewing. The Clark company later merged with J. & P. Coats. "O.N.T.," which appeared on many posters and postcard advertisements for Spool Cotton, stood for "Our New Thread."

Finishing the Edges

The edge treatment is an important part of the quilt design as well as a factor contributing to the durability of the quilt. Make your fabric calculations with the binding or other edge finish in mind.

For my replicas of antique quilts, I choose to use bindings rather than hemmed edges because of the durability that binding provides. I choose colors consistent with the edge finishes of the quilts. I use both straight grain and bias bindings.

Finish a straight edge without binding by bringing the quilt top to the back or the backing to the front, turning under the raw edge and blindstitching it in place. Miter the corners as you work. This method works only if you have planned ahead and allowed enough excess fabric to turn to the other side.

Self-Binding

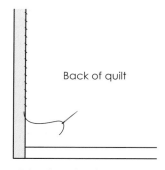

Back of quilt

Bring front fabric to back.

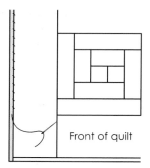

Front of quilt

Bring backing to front.

If you plan to bring the backing forward, consider the impact of the backing color on the finished quilt top. Also, with only one layer of fabric to take the wear, the edges of many old quilts with finishes of this type are worn through. A double binding is a sturdier edge treatment.

Straight-grain bindings are more common on quilts made before the 1920s, before designs with scalloped edges became popular. Bias binding makes a smoother finish on curved edges.

You can sew decorative piping into a bias finish if you wish. (See Stars and Ninepatches on page 48.) Ruffles or folded squares called "prairie points" may also be added to decorate edges.

Quilts with irregular edges may require facing for a smooth finish. The Sunshine and Shadow version of Trip Around the World, the pieced "ice cream cone" border, and some Flower Garden edges finish more easily with a facing.

Applying a Facing

1. Baste the edges of the quilt together and trim evenly.

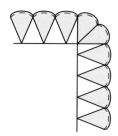

Baste and trim quilt top batting and backing together.

2. Cut a strip of the backing fabric just wider than the unit forming the edge. Layer the right side of the quilt on the right side of the fabric strip. Stitch a ¼"-wide seam following the shape of the outer edge.

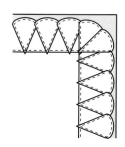

Layer right sides of facing and quilt together. Stitch along border edge.

3. Pivot at the seam intersections; lift the presser foot with the needle down. When the stitching is complete, trim the facing fabric to match the top.

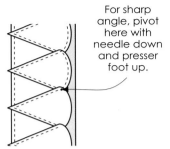

For sharp angle, pivot here with needle down and presser foot up.

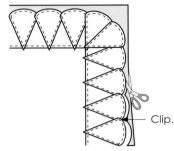

Clip.

Trim away facing fabric.

4. Turn the facing strip to the back of the quilt, making sure the shapes are smooth. Turn the edge of the facing strip under and blindstitch to the back of the quilt.

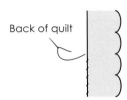

Back of quilt

Another vintage quilt technique for irregular edges is referred to as "hemming together" or a "knife edge." Cut the backing to the shape and size of the top and fold the edge of the quilt top under ¼". Fold under the same amount on the edge of the backing fabric. Join the layers with blind stitches or tiny buttonhole stitches. No color from the back shows on the front, and no fabric from the front shows on the back with this method.

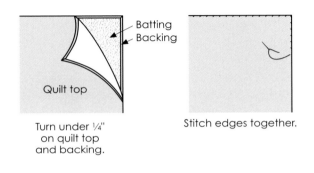

Batting
Backing

Quilt top

Turn under ¼" on quilt top and backing.

Stitch edges together.

Making Rotary-Cut Bias Binding

The following instructions are by Jackie Reis of Accu-Pattern Drafting Service.

When you need more than a one-yard length of bias binding, use a calculator and the following method to determine the size of the square needed.

1. Find the distance, in inches, around the quilt: two lengths plus two widths.
2. Add 10" for overlap and curves or mitering corners.
3. Multiply this number by the width of the binding you plan to cut.
4. Push the "square root" symbol on the calculator. Round the answer to the next highest whole number and add the width of the binding you plan to cut.

For example: The quilt measures 90" x 108".

90" + 108" = 198" (length plus width)
198" x 2 = 396" (distance around quilt)
396" + 10" (perimeter plus allowance) = 406"
406" x 2 (width to cut binding) = 812"

Square root of 812 = 28.4956. Round to 29.
29" + 2" = 31". A 31" square of binding fabric is required.

Follow these steps to cut bias binding.

1. Cut a square of binding fabric the required size. Cut it in half diagonally.

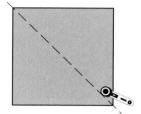

2. Place the pieces right sides together as shown. With edges even, stitch by machine, using a ⅜"-wide seam allowance. Press the seam open.

3. Place the fabric on the cutting board with the wrong side of the fabric touching the board and the bias edges parallel to the length of the board.

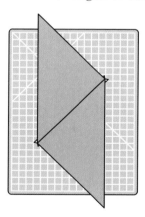

4. Fold the upper tip of fabric down to the seam line and fold the lower tip up to the seam line so the straight-grain edges meet diagonally but do not overlap. This is the butting line.

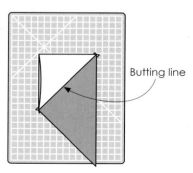

Butting line

5. Keep the bias edges even on the left side, and as even as possible on the right. (Left-handed users, reverse these directions.) Begin cutting the desired binding width from the left (lefties on the right), using a rotary cutter, mat, and acrylic ruler. Stop the cutting 1" before the seam line and start again 1" after it so the cut will jump the line. Continue to cut across the width of the fabric with parallel cuts, jumping across the seam line on each cut. Cut through and discard the last incomplete row.

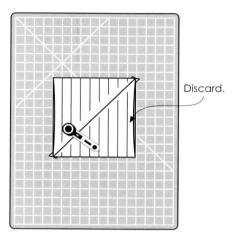

Discard.

6. Gently lift up the tip of the first row and use scissors to cut through to the end of the fabric (A+). Gently lift up the tip of the last row and cut through to the end of fabric (B).

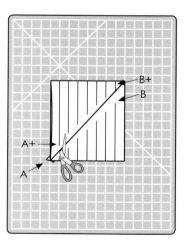

B+
B
A+
A

Gently slide and align the fabrics at the seam line so that A is even with A+ and B is even with B+.

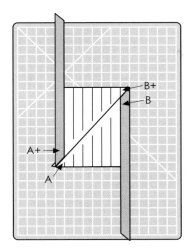

7. With right sides together, join butted edges with a ⅜"-wide seam allowance to form a tube.
8. Slide the fabric tube over the ironing board; press the seam open. Using fabric scissors, cut across the uncut portions of fabric, making a long, continuous strip.

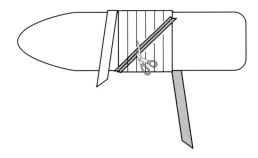

9. Unwind the bias strip from the ironing board.
10. For doubled binding, press the strip in half lengthwise with wrong sides together.

Attaching Binding with Mitered Corners

1. Place the binding, right sides together, along the raw edge of the layered quilt. Sew the binding to the quilt, using a ¼"-wide seam allowance. Stitch the binding to within ¼" of the quilt-top edge. Backstitch to anchor the binding at that point.

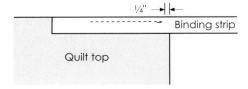

Backstitch ¼" from edge.

2. Fold the binding to the back of the quilt and finger crease the binding at the fold.

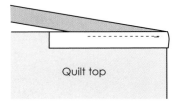

Crease binding.

3. Bring the creased fold to the top edge of the quilt corner, then turn down so raw edge is even with the adjacent quilt edge. Begin stitching where the previous stitching stopped. Backstitch to anchor.

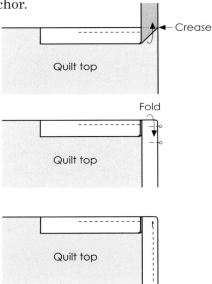

4. Continue sewing binding to the quilt edges, repeating these mitering steps at each of the remaining corners.
5. Bring the binding edge to the back of the quilt. On the front it will form a miter at each corner.

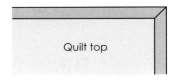

6. On the back of the quilt, fold one side of the binding over the other and stitch to the backing as shown.

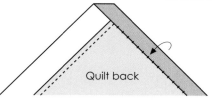

Joining Binding Ends with a Diagonal Seam

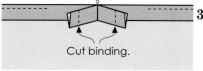

1. Stop stitching about 8" from the point where you began sewing the binding to the quilt. Tails should overlap several inches. Insert a straight pin into the quilt in the middle of the space between where the stitching begins and ends.

2. Pin the strips together, but not to the quilt, at the point where the pin is in the quilt. The binding should fit comfortably along the unsewn edge. Remove pin from quilt.

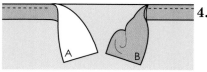
Cut binding.

3. Measuring from the binding pin, cut the strips one-half the width of the binding. (If binding is cut 2" wide, each strip is cut 1" from the pin.)

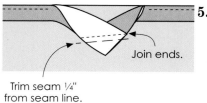

4. Remove the binding pin, open left strip wrong side up (A), and open right strip right side up (B).

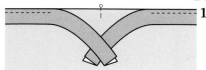
Join ends.

Trim seam ¼" from seam line.

5. Place end A at a right angle to, and on top of, end B. Stitch diagonally across the ends to form a triangle. Trim off excess triangle of seam allowance.

6. Open binding; finger press seam open. Refold on fold line if using a doubled binding. The length of the unsewn binding should match the unsewn distance on the quilt. Stitch binding to quilt.

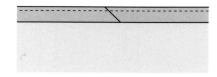

7. Using thread to match binding, hand stitch binding to quilt back.

Signing and Dating Your Quilt

Signing your quilt can be as simple as writing your name with a permanent fabric pen or as elaborate as your stitching skills allow. The more information you provide about yourself and your quilt at the time you finish it, the better for your descendants and future quilt historians.

Include your name as quiltmaker (not just initials) and list your maiden name (often forgotten until the genealogy bug bites). Add the date the quilt was finished, and the city and state in which the quilt was made. Add other information, such as the name of the pattern, the source of the design, or the name of the person for whom the quilt was made.

You can use embroidered or cross-stitched labels. Printed labels are also available for today's quiltmakers to record name, date, place, occasion, and so on. Permanent pens and detailed instructions allow personalized labels, and some books show you how to draw your own labels.

Finding a name and date on an antique quilt may require hours of searching in the quilting. You may enjoy quilting your name into your quilt, and the fun may be in deciding how to disguise the letters in the quilting stitches.

All of the quiltmakers who remain anonymous in this book would have been named if they had signed their quilts years ago.

Appendix

Quilt Backings

Cutting and seaming options for backings are shown below. Backings for the quilts in this book were planned to utilize the smallest possible amount of fabric. Small quilts have a one-piece backing. Unless otherwise marked, larger backings require two or three lengths of fabric.

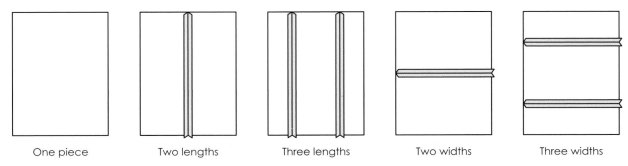

| One piece | Two lengths | Three lengths | Two widths | Three widths |

Side-by-Side Settings

This chart provides finished quilt sizes plus backing and binding yardage for side-by-side settings of blocks in four sizes. Use with vintage or new blocks.

10" Blocks

Size	Wall/Crib	Twin	Double	Queen	King
No. of Blocks	4 x 5	6 x 9	8 x 10	9 x 10	11 x 11
Finished Size	40" x 50"	60" x 90"	80" x 100"	90" x 100"	110" x 110"
Backing Yardage	1⅝	5¼	6	8**	10
Binding Yardage	½	¾	1	1	1

12" Blocks

Size	Wall/Crib	Twin	Double	Queen	King
No. of Blocks	3 x 4	5 x 7	7 x 8	8 x 9	9 x 9
Finished Size	36" x 48"	60" x 84"	84" x 96"	96" x 108"	108" x 108"
Backing Yardage	1½	3½	5¾	8½**	9½
Binding Yardage	½	¾	1	1	1

14" Blocks

Size	Wall/Crib	Twin	Double	Queen	King
No. of Blocks	3 x 4	4 x 7	6 x 7	7 x 8	8 x 8
Finished Size	42" x 56"	56" x 98"	84" x 98"	98" x 112"	112" x 112"
Backing Yardage	1¾	5¾	6	8½**	9¾
Binding Yardage	½	¾	1	1	1

16" Blocks

Size	Wall/Crib	Twin	Double	Queen	King
No. of Blocks	**3 x 4**	**4 x 5**	**5 x 6**	**6 x 7**	**7 x 7**
Finished Size	48" x 64"	64" x 80"	80" x 96"	96" x 112"	112" x 112"
Backing Yardage	1¾	4*	6	8½**	9¾
Binding Yardage	½	¾	1	1	1

*Use two fabric widths. See quilt backing illustration on page 75.
**Use three fabric widths. See quilt backing illustration on page 75.

Lattice Settings

Use this chart when planning quilts set with a lattice. The chart lists the number of short (A), horizontal (B), and outer (C) lattice strips for different numbers of blocks. The placement of A, B, and C are shown on this standard lattice plan.

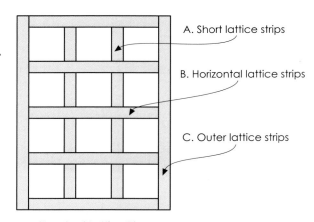

A. Short lattice strips

B. Horizontal lattice strips

C. Outer lattice strips

Standard Lattice Plan

Number of Lattice Pieces to Cut

No. of Blocks	3 x 3	3 x 4	3 x 5	4 x 4	4 x 5	4 x 6	5 x 5	5 x 6	5 x 7	6 x 6
Short Strips (A)	6	8	10	12	15	18	20	24	28	30
Horizontal Strips (B)	4	5	6	5	6	7	6	7	8	7
Outer Strips (C)	2	2	2	2	2	2	2	2	2	2

No. of Blocks	6 x 7	6 x 8	7 x 7	7 x 8	7 x 9	8 x 8	8 x 9	9 x 9	10 x 10
Short Strips (A)	35	40	42	48	54	56	63	72	90
Horizontal Strips (B)	8	9	8	9	10	9	10	10	11
Outer Strips (C)	2	2	2	2	2	2	2	2	2

Straight Lattice Settings

This chart lists quilt sizes and yardage for lattice strips in several widths for 10", 12", 14", and 16" blocks. Use with the "Lattice Settings" chart on page 76.

Planning for 10" Blocks

Straight Lattice Setting

Size	Wall/Crib	Twin	Double	Queen	King
No. of Blocks	**3 x 4**	**5 x 8**	**7 x 8**	**8 x 9**	**9 x 9**
1½" Lattice	36" x 47½"	59" x 93½"	82" x 93½"	93½" x 105"	105" x 105"
Lattice Yardage	1½	2¾	2¾	3¼	3¼
No. of Blocks	**3 x 4**	**5 x 8**	**7 x 8**	**8 x 9**	**9 x 9**
2" Lattice	38" x 50"	62" x 98"	86" x 98"	98" x 110"	110" x 110"
Lattice Yardage	1⅝	2⅞	3	3⅓	3⅓
No. of Blocks	**3 x 4**	**5 x 7**	**6 x 8**	**7 x 8**	**8 x 8**
2½" Lattice	40" x 52½"	65" x 90"	77½" x 102½"	90" x 102½"	102½" x 102½"
Lattice Yardage	1⅝	2¾	3¼	3¼	3¼
No. of Blocks	**3 x 4**	**5 x 7**	**6 x 7**	**7 x 8**	**8 x 8**
3" Lattice	42" x 55"	68" x 94"	81" x 94"	94" x 101"	107" x 107"
Lattice Yardage	1⅔	2⅞	2⅞	3	3⅓

Planning for 12" Blocks

Straight Lattice Setting

Size	Wall/Crib	Twin	Double	Queen	King
No. of Blocks	**3 x 4**	**4 x 6**	**6 x 7**	**6 x 7**	**8 x 8**
2" Lattice	44" x 58"	58" x 86"	86" x 100"	86" x 100"	114" x 114"
Lattice Yardage	1¾	3½	3	3	3⅓
No. of Blocks	**3 x 4**	**4 x 6**	**6 x 7**	**6 x 7**	**8 x 8**
2½" Lattice	46" x 60½"	60½" x 89½"	89½" x 104"	89½" x 104"	118½" x 118½"
Lattice Yardage	1⅞	2¾	3¼	3¼	3½
No. of Blocks	**3 x 4**	**4 x 6**	**5 x 6**	**6 x 7**	**7 x 7**
3" Lattice	48" x 63"	63" x 93"	78" x 96"	96" x 111"	111" x 111"
Lattice Yardage	2	2¾	3	3⅓	4¼
No. of Blocks	**3 x 4**	**4 x 6**	**6 x 7**	**6 x 7**	**7 x 7**
3½" Lattice	50" x 65½"	65½" x 86½"	86½" x 112"	86½" x 112"	112" x 112"
Lattice Yardage	2	3	4½	4½	4½

�� ✦ **NOTE** ✦ ✦ ✦ ✦

Additional borders may be added to further enlarge the quilt.

Planning for 14" Blocks

Straight Lattice Setting

Size	Wall/Crib	Twin	Double	Queen	King
No. of Blocks	3 x 4	4 x 6	5 x 6	5 x 7	7 x 7
2" Lattice	50" x 66"	66" x 98"	82" x 98"	82" x 114"	114" x 114"
Lattice Yardage	2	3	3	3¼	3¼
No. of Blocks		4 x 5	5 x 6	5 x 6	7 x 7
2½" Lattice		68½" x 85"	85" x 101½"	85" x 101½"	118" x 118"
Lattice Yardage		2½	3	3	3½
No. of Blocks		3 x 5	5 x 6	5 x 6	6 x 6
3" Lattice		54" x 88"	88" x 105"	88" x 105"	105" x 105"
Lattice Yardage		2⅔	3¼	3¼	4½
No. of Blocks		3 x 5	4 x 5	5 x 6	6 x 6
3½" Lattice		56" x 91"	73½" x 91"	91" x 118½"	108½" x 108½"
Lattice Yardage		2¾	2¾	3½	4

Planning for 16" Blocks

Straight Lattice Setting

Size	Twin	Double	Queen	King
No. of Blocks	3 x 5	4 x 5	5 x 6	6 x 6
2½" Lattice	58" x 95"	76½" x 95"	95" x 113½"	113½" x 113½"
Lattice Yardage	2¾	2¾	3¼	3¼
No. of Blocks	3 x 5	5 x 6	5 x 6	6 x 6
3" Lattice	60" x 98"	79" x 98"	98" x 117"	117" x 117"
Lattice Yardage	3	3	3⅓	3⅓
No. of Blocks	3 x 5	4 x 5	5 x 5	5 x 5
3½" Lattice	62" x 101"	81½" x 101"	101" x 101"	101" x 101"
Lattice Yardage	3	3	3	3
No. of Blocks	3 x 5	4 x 5	4 x 5	5 x 5
4" Lattice	64" x 104"	84" x 104"	84" x 104"	104" x 104"
Lattice Yardage	3	3½	3½	3½

Diagonal Measurements

Use this chart when you need to know the diagonal measurement of a square. Remember the diagonal measure of a square is 1.414 times the side of the square. The fraction equivalents have been rounded up.

SQUARE	DIAGONAL
1"	1½"
2"	2⅞"
3"	4¼"
4"	5⅝"
5"	7⅛"
6"	8½"
7"	9⅞"
8"	11⅓"
9"	12¾"
10"	14⅛"
11"	15⅔"
12"	17"
13"	18⅓"
14"	19⅞"
15"	21¼"
16"	22⅝"
17"	24"
18"	25½"
20"	28¼"
22"	31⅛"
24"	34"

Diagonal Settings

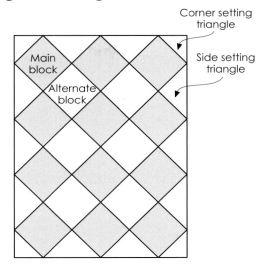

Corner setting triangle

Side setting triangle

Main block

Alternate block

Use this chart to determine the number of blocks in a diagonally set quilt.

Arrangement	Main Blocks	Alternate Blocks	Side Setting Triangles	Corner Setting Triangles
2 x 2	4	1	4	4
2 x 3	6	2	6	4
3 x 3	9	4	8	4
3 x 4	12	6	10	4
3 x 5	15	8	12	4
4 x 4	16	9	12	4
4 x 5	20	12	14	4
4 x 6	24	15	16	4
5 x 5	25	16	16	4
5 x 6	30	20	18	4
5 x 7	35	24	20	4
6 x 6	36	25	20	4
6 x 7	42	30	22	4
6 x 8	48	35	24	4
7 x 7	49	36	24	4
7 x 8	56	42	26	4
7 x 9	63	48	28	4
8 x 8	64	49	28	4
8 x 9	72	56	30	4
9 x 9	81	64	32	4
9 x 10	90	72	36	4
10 x 10	100	81	36	4
10 x 12	120	99	40	4
11 x 11	121	100	40	4
12 x 12	144	121	44	4

Side and Corner Triangles

Use this chart to determine the sizes of side and corner triangles to fill in diagonal settings or to finish Star blocks.[10]

Finished Block Size	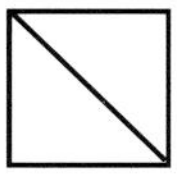 Cut Square Size for Corner Triangle	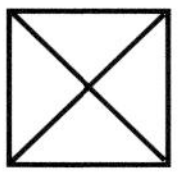 Cut Square Size for Side Triangle
2" Block	2⅜"	4⅛"
3" Block	3"	5½"
4" Block	3¾"	7"
5" Block	4½"	8⅜"
6" Block	5⅛"	9¾"
7" Block	5⅞"	11¼"
8" Block	6⅝"	12⅝"
9" Block	7¼"	14"
10" Block	8"	15½"
12" Block	9⅜"	18¼"
14" Block	10⅞"	21⅛"
16" Block	12¼"	23⅞"
18" Block	13⅝"	26¾"
20" Block	15⅛"	29⅝"
24" Block	17⅞"	35¼"

Double Wedding Ring Quilts

Refer to this chart to find the number of pieces required for a certain ring setting or to determine a setting for the pieces you have.

Bands	Set	Centers	Ovals
48	3 x 3	9	24
62	3 x 4	12	31
76	3 x 5	15	38
98	4 x 5	20	49
116	4 x 6	24	58
142	5 x 6	30	71
164	5 x 7	35	82
194	6 x 7	42	97
220	6 x 8	48	110
252	7 x 8	56	126
284	7 x 9	63	142
322	8 x 9	72	161

Tools and Supplies

Today there are many wonderful tools and supplies that were not available to quiltmakers of the past. Use these to make your work easier and more accurate.

Rotary Cutter and Mat

Purchase the largest mat you can conveniently use and store. Treat yourself to a small mat for cutting scraps.

Make a habit of closing your rotary cutter when it is not in use. Keep your cutter in good shape by cleaning it regularly. Loosen the screw and keep the pieces in order. Wipe away the lint with a soft cotton cloth and smooth on a drop of oil. Reassemble the cutter in reverse order. Keep a replacement blade in reserve.

Rulers

Choose rulers made of clear, hard acrylic, specifically designed for use with rotary cutters. Handy rulers to have are:

6" or 8" Bias Square. Use this to check corners and right angles and to square up blocks.

The ScrapMaster. This ruler is designed for cutting individual half-square triangles in a variety of sizes from scraps.

6" x 24" acrylic ruler. This is helpful for cutting strips and borders.

12½" or larger square acrylic ruler. This is useful for sizing vintage blocks.

Sewing Machine

Clean and adjust your machine before starting a new project. Use a 70/10 or 80/20 needle with a universal point. It is now my habit to remove the throat plate and clean the "fuzzies" each time I put in a new bobbin. Cotton thread makes lint, and lint stops up the machine if it is not removed regularly. If cleaning at every bobbin change sounds often, do it after every two bobbins, and you will see how much lint accumulates. Prepare several bobbins ahead in order to keep sewing without repeated interruptions to wind bobbins.

Needles

For hand quilting, use #9 or #10 Betweens; for hand appliqué, use a #12 Sharp. A #8 embroidery needle will carry floss for hand embroidery.

Pins

Keep plenty of fine straight pins on hand. The heavier pins make holes in vintage fabrics. I like having two containers so that one can be at the sewing machine and one at the ironing board.

You need 200–300 size #1 nickel-plated safety pins for pin-basting the layers of a quilt together for quilting.

Iron and Ironing Board

Use a steam/dry iron and a spray water bottle. Keep an eye on the condition of the iron plate so that no dye transfers from fabric to fabric. When pressing vintage fabrics, use a layer of old sheeting to protect your ironing board cover.

Marking Tools

A .5 mechanical pencil draws fine seam lines. A silver marking pencil is good for marking quilting lines. Tracing paper and graph paper in several scales help in planning quilts made from vintage blocks. If you choose to make templates for some of the quilts, you will need template plastic.

Washing Products

Orvus and Ensure can be used safely to wash vintage fabrics.

Notes

1. Newman, *Quilts of the Texas South Plains*, p. 16.
2. Lasansky, *In the Heart of Pennsylvania*, p. 42.
3. Newman, *Quilts of the Texas South Plains*, p. 16.
4. Arkansas Quilter's Guild, *Arkansas Quilts*, p. 128.
5. Beyer, *The Art and Technique of Creating Medallion Quilts*, p. 63.
6. Peto, *Historic Quilts*, p. 153.
7. Meller and Elffers, *Textile Designs*, p. 88.
8. Voris, *The New Columbian White House Cookery*, p. 478.
9. Finley, *Old Patchwork Quilts and the Women Who Made Them*, p. 146.
10. Hanson, *Sensational Settings*, p. 53.

Quilt Styles

The following references list publications that contain quilts of the same style or period as those described in this book.

Garden Maze Setting
Arkansas Quilter's Guild, Inc., *Arkansas Quilts*, Oak Leaf and Reel, p. 66.
Frost, Helen Young and Stevenson, Pam Knight, *Grand Endeavors, Vintage Arizona Quilts and Their Makers*, Double Ninepatch, p. 184; Feathered Star, p. 149; Compass and Chain, p. 36.
Lasansky, Jeannette, *Pieced by Mother*, Myers quilt, pp. 58, 59.

Lone Star
Lasansky, Jeannette, *Pieced by Mother*, Bethlehem Star, pp. 76–77.
Cockran, Erickson, Hart and Schaffer, *New Jersey Quilts 1777 to 1950*, Lone Star with Broderie Perse, p. 41; Lone Star with Feathered Edge, p. 72.
Cooper and Buferd, *The Quilters, Women and Domestic Art*, Lone Star, p. 72.
Irwin, John Rice, *A People and Their Quilts*, Lone Star, pp. 73, 74, 170.
Levie, Place, and Sears, *Country Living's Country Quilts*, Radiant Star, p. 61.

Medallion Style Quilts:
Heidingsfelder, Sharon, *Quilts*, p. 26.

Pattern Quilts
Lasansky, Jeannette, *Pieced by Mother 1987*, Sechler sampler top, p. 40.
Lasansky, Jeannette, *Pieced by Mother 1988*, sampler quilt top, p. 110; Hettinger sampler quilt top, p. 113.
Martin, Nancy J., *Threads of Time*, 1890 Sampler, p. 56.
Rogers Historical Museum, *Stitches in Time, A Legacy of Ozark Quilts*, Pattern Sampler, cover.

Stars and Ninepatches
Cockran, Erickson, Hart and Schaffer, *New Jersey Quilts 1777 to 1950*, Starburst with Eight Pointed Stars, p. 17; Double X, p. 75.

Triple Lattice
Arkansas Quilter's Guild, Inc., *Arkansas Quilts*, Dutch Doll, p. 134; Dutch Doll, p. 136; Butterfly, p. 137.
Levie, Place, and Sears, *Country Living's Country Quilts*, Jacob's Ladder, p. 101.
Newman, Sharon, ed., *Quilts of the Texas South Plains*, Sagebud, p. 16.

Wide Lattice in Third Quarter of the 19th Century

Arkansas Quilter's Guild, *Arkansas Quilts,* Eight-Point Star, p. 20; Ocean Wave variation, p. 30.

Holstein, Jonathan, *Abstract Design in American Quilts,* Four Patch Block, p. 169.

Holstein, Jonathan, *The Pieced Quilt: An American Design Tradition,* Crazy Stars, plate 79; Crazy blocks, plate 80.

Lasansky, Jeannette, *Pieced by Mother,* Heiser quilt, p. 61.

Nelson, Cyril I. *Quilt Engagement Calendar 1979,* Snow Crystals, plate 21.

Bibliography

Arkansas Quilter's Guild. *Arkansas Quilts.* Paducah, Ky.: American Quilter's Society, 1987.

Beyer, Jinny. *The Art and Technique of Creating Medallion Quilts.* McLean, Va.: EPM Publications, Inc., 1982.

Brackman, Barbara. *Encyclopedia of Pieced Quilt Patterns.* Lawrence, Kan.: Prairie Flower Publishing, 1984.

———. *Clues in the Calico.* McLean, Va.: EPM Publications, Inc., 1989.

Cockran, Erickson, Hart and Schaffer. *New Jersey Quilts.* Paducah, Ky.: American Quilter's Society, 1992.

Cooper and Buferd. *The Quilter's Women and Domestic Art.* Garden City, N.Y.: Doubleday and Company, Inc., 1977.

Finley, Ruth E. *Old Patchwork Quilts and the Women Who Made Them.* Newton Center, Mass.: Charles T. Branford Company, 1929.

Frost, Helen Young, and Pam Knight Stevenson. *Grand Endeavors, Vintage Arizona Quilts and Their Makers.* Flagstaff, Ariz.: Northland Publishing Company, 1992.

Garoutte, Sally, ed., *Uncoverings, 1983.* Mill Valley, Calif.: American Quilt Study Group, 1983.

Goldman, Marilyn, and Marguerite Wiebusch. *Quilts of Indiana, Crossroads of Memories.* Bloomington and Indianapolis, Ind.: Indiana University Press, 1991.

Gutcheon, Jeff. *A Quilter's Guide to Printed Fabric.* Tacoma, Wash.: Gutcheon Patchworks, Inc., 1990.

Hall, Carrie A., and Rose G. Kretsinger. *The Romance of the Patchwork Quilt in America.* New York: Bonanza Books, 1935.

Hanson, Joan. *Sensational Settings.* Bothell, Wash.: That Patchwork Place, 1993.

Heidingsfelder, Sharon. *Quilts.* Little Rock, Ark.: University of Arkansas Cooperative Extension Service.

Holstein, Jonathan. *Abstract Design in American Quilts: A Biography of an Exhibition.* Louisville, Ky.: The Kentucky Quilt Project, 1991.

———. *The Pieced Quilt: An American Design Tradition.* Greenwich, Conn.: New York Graphic Society, Ltd., 1973.

Irwin, John Rice. *A People and Their Quilts.* Exton, Pa.: Schiffer Publishing Limited, 1984.

Jenkins, Susan, and Linda Seward. *The American Quilt Story.* Emmaus, Pa.: Rodale Press, 1991.

Lasansky, Jeannette. *Bits and Pieces.* Lewisburg, Pa.: Oral Traditions Project of the Union County Historical Society, 1991.

———. *In the Heart of Pennsylvania.* Lewisburg, Pa.: Oral Traditions Project of the Union County Historical Society, 1985.

———. *Pieced by Mother.* Lewisburg, Pa.: Oral Traditions Project of the Union County Historical Society, 1987.

————. *Pieced by Mother*. Lewisburg, Pa.: Oral Traditions Project of the Union County Historical Society, 1988.

Levie, Place, and Sears. *Country Living's Country Quilts*. New York: Hearst Books, 1992.

Martin, Nancy J. *Threads of Time*. Bothell, Wash.: That Patchwork Place, 1990.

McMorris, Penny. *Crazy Quilts*. New York: E.P. Dutton, 1984.

Meller, Susan, and Joost Elffers. *Textile Designs*. New York: Harry N. Abrams, Inc., 1991.

Nelson, Cyril I. *Quilt Engagement Calendar*. New York: E.P. Dutton, 1979.

Newman, Sharon, ed., *Quilts of the Texas South Plains*. Lubbock, Tex.: Prairie Windmill Publishing, 1986.

Orlofsky, Patsy and Myron. *Quilts in America*. New York: McGraw-Hill Book Company, 1974.

Peto, Florence. *American Quilts and Coverlets*. New York: Webster, Chanticleer Press, 1949.

————. *Historic Quilts*. New York: The American Historical Company, Inc., 1939.

Rehmel, Judy. *The Quilt I. D. Book*. New York: Prentice Hall Press, 1986.

Rogers Historical Museum. *Stitches in Time, A Legacy of Ozark Quilts*. Rogers, Ark.: Rogers Historical Museum, 1986.

Voris, Emma Frances. *The New Columbian White House Cookery*. Chicago, Ill.: A. B. Kuhlam & Company, copyrighted by Charles S. Sutphen, 1893.

Webster, Marie D. *Quilts: Their Story and How to Make Them*. New edition. Santa Barbara, Calif.: Practical Patchwork, 1990.

Woodard, Thomas K., and Blanch Greenstein. *Twentieth Century Quilts 1900–1950*. New York: E.P. Dutton, 1988.

Sunbonnet Sue
Placement Template

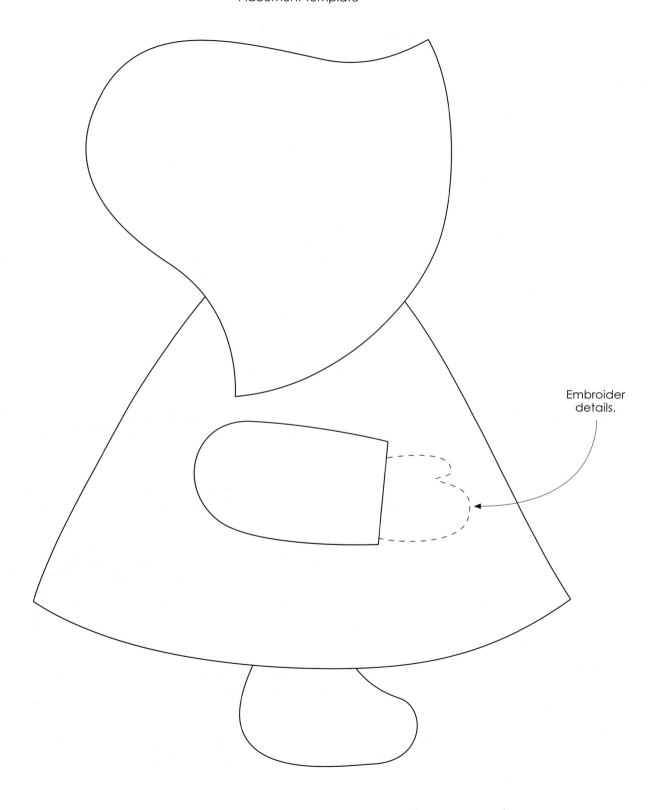

Embroider
details.

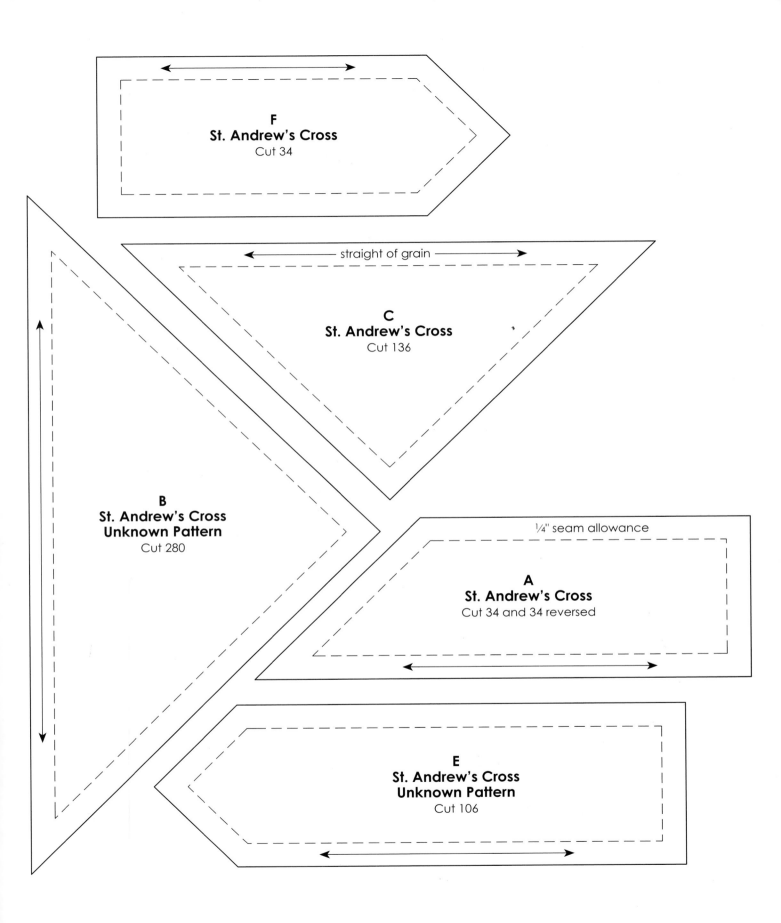

F
St. Andrew's Cross
Cut 34

straight of grain

C
St. Andrew's Cross
Cut 136

B
St. Andrew's Cross
Unknown Pattern
Cut 280

¼" seam allowance

A
St. Andrew's Cross
Cut 34 and 34 reversed

E
St. Andrew's Cross
Unknown Pattern
Cut 106

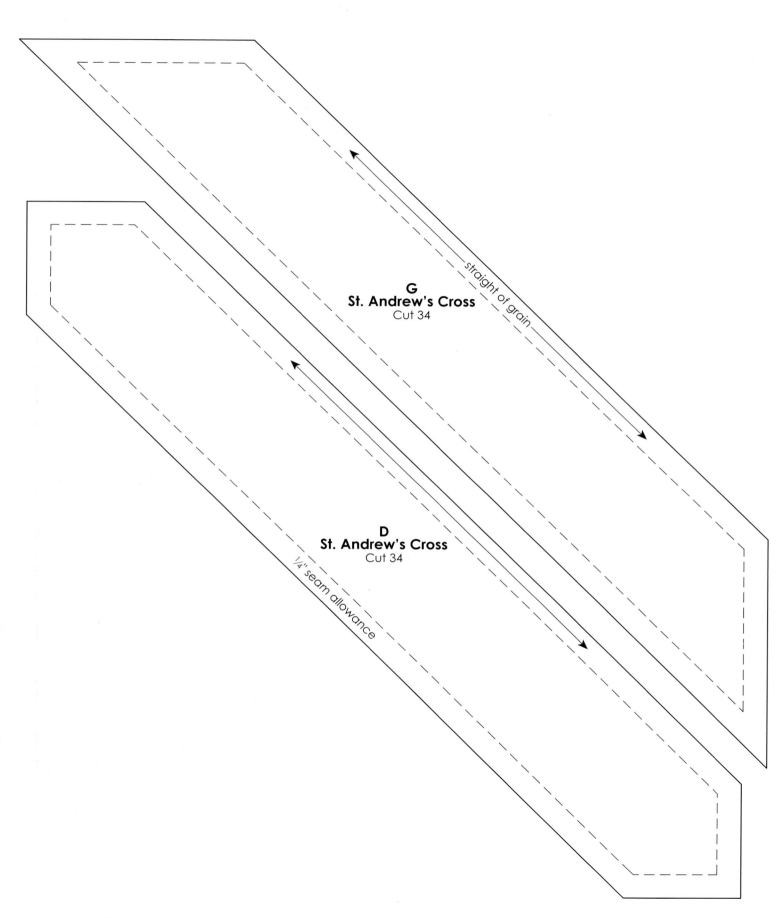

G
St. Andrew's Cross
Cut 34

straight of grain

D
St. Andrew's Cross
Cut 34

¼" seam allowance

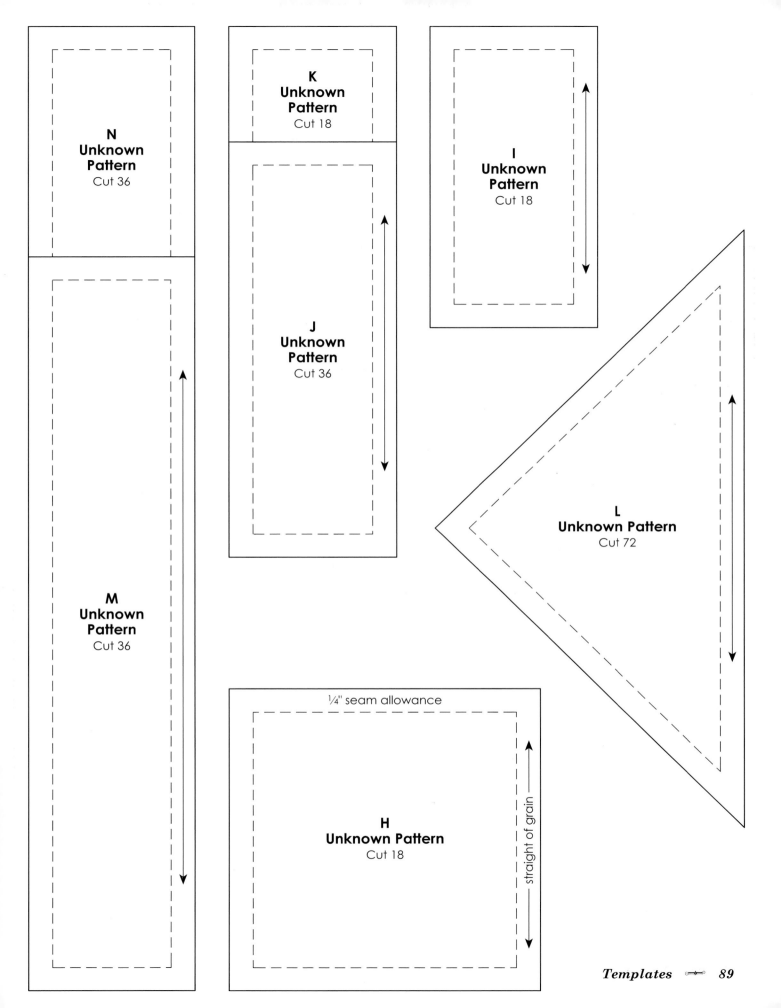

N
Unknown Pattern
Cut 36

K
Unknown Pattern
Cut 18

I
Unknown Pattern
Cut 18

J
Unknown Pattern
Cut 36

L
Unknown Pattern
Cut 72

M
Unknown Pattern
Cut 36

¼" seam allowance

H
Unknown Pattern
Cut 18

straight of grain

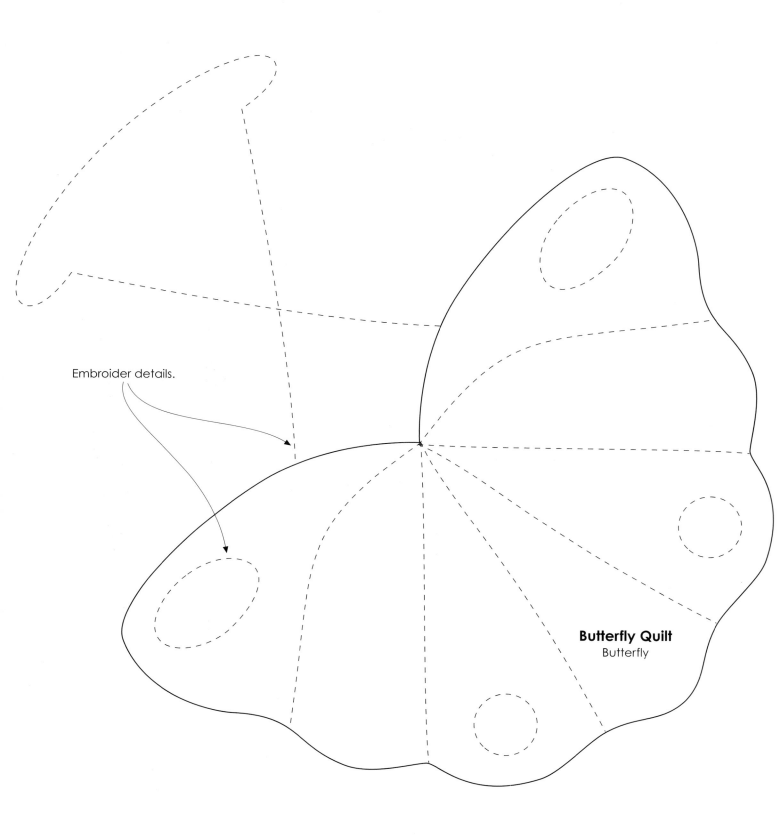

Embroider details.

Butterfly Quilt
Butterfly

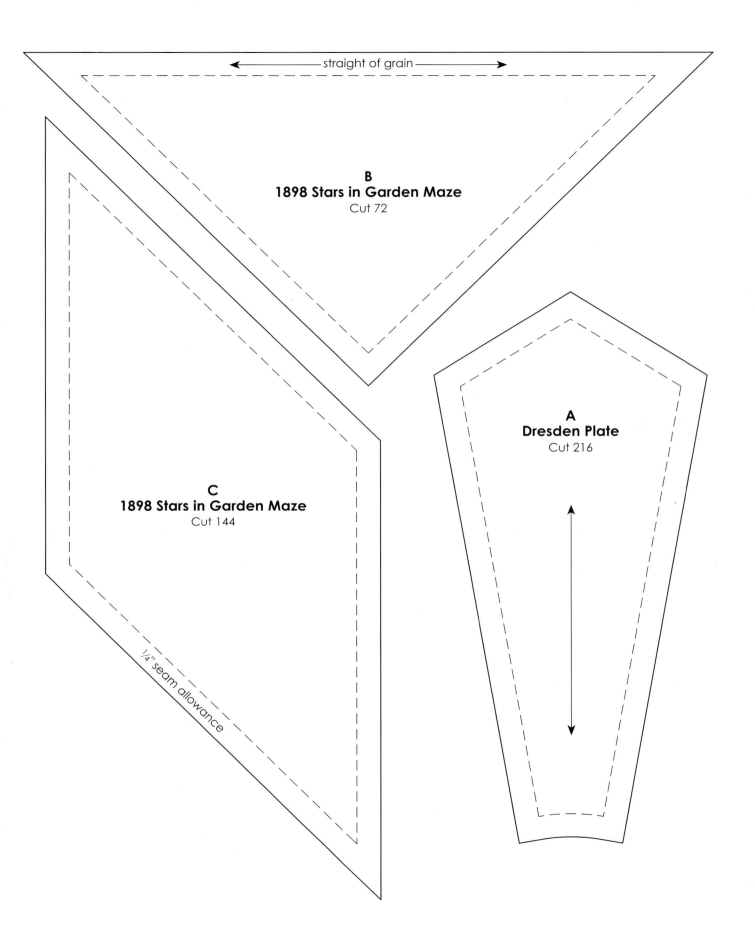

straight of grain

B
1898 Stars in Garden Maze
Cut 72

C
1898 Stars in Garden Maze
Cut 144

¼" seam allowance

A
Dresden Plate
Cut 216

straight of grain

A
1898 Stars in Garden Maze
Cut 84

¼" seam allowance

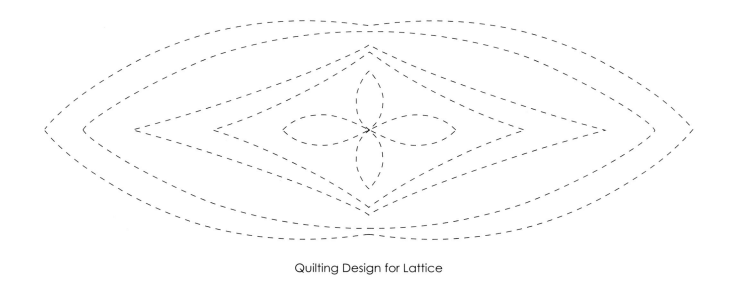

Quilting Design for Lattice

B
Cameo Tulips
Tulip
Cut 1 for each block

C
Cameo Tulips
Tulip
Cut 1 for each block

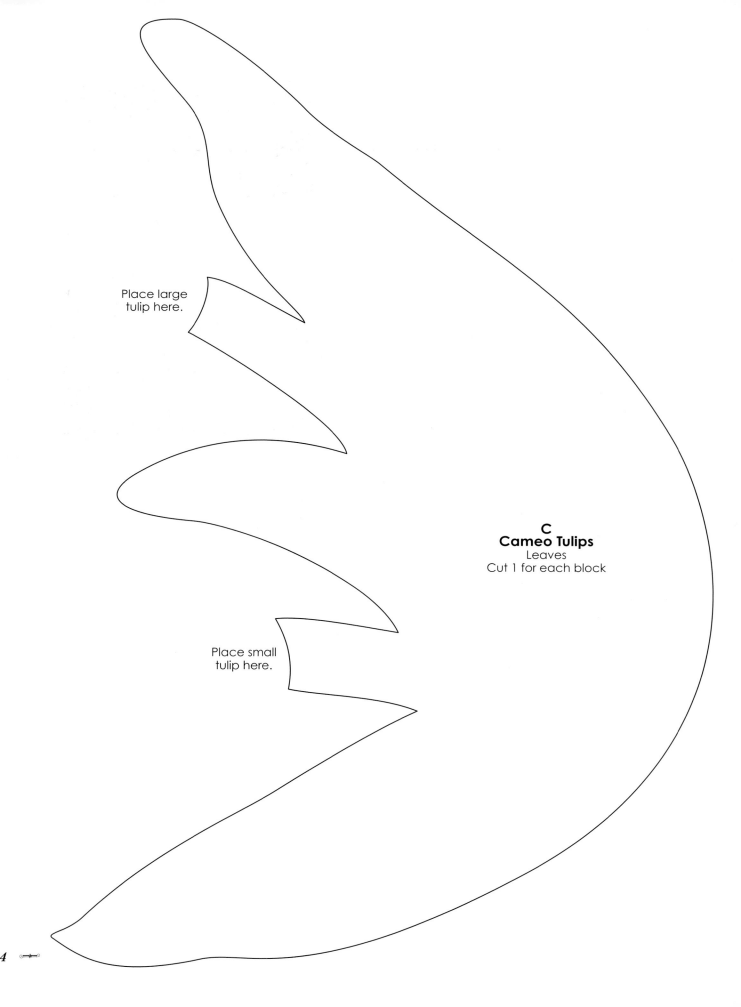

Place large
tulip here.

C
Cameo Tulips
Leaves
Cut 1 for each block

Place small
tulip here.

About the Author

Sharon L. Newman opened The Quilt Shop in Lubbock, Texas, in January 1979. In addition to teaching quiltmaking and presenting lectures about quilts and quilters, she appraises quilts and currently serves as administrator for the American Quilter's Society Appraisal Certification Program.

A charter member of both The American Quilter's Society and the American International Quilt Association, Sharon is also a member of the National Quilting Association and the Quilter's Guild of Dallas. She was a founding member of the South Plains Quilter's Guild and the Chaparral Quilter's Guild, both in Lubbock.

Sharon was curator for the 1986 Texas Sesquicentennial Quilt Exhibit in the Ranching Heritage Center, Texas Tech University, and editor of the exhibit catalog, "Quilts of the Texas South Plains." She is the author of *Handkerchief Quilts*, published in 1992.

Sharon was born and reared in Indiana. She is a graduate of the University of Texas, Austin, with a teaching degree in mathematics and English. She and her husband, Thomas, have lived in Lubbock since 1967. They have three daughters; Tracy Faulkner, Vicki Potts, and Carol Newman; one grandson, Clinton Thomas Faulkner, and one granddaughter, Taylor Alexandra Faulkner.

That Patchwork Place Publications and Products

All the Blocks Are Geese
   by Mary Sue Suit
Angle Antics by Mary Hickey
Animas Quilts by Jackie Robinson
Appliqué Borders: An Added Grace
   by Jeana Kimball
Appliqué in Bloom by Gabrielle Swain
Appliquilt: Whimsical One-Step Appliqué
   by Tonee White
Around the Block with Judy Hopkins
Baltimore Bouquets by Mimi Dietrich
Bargello Quilts by Marge Edie
Basket Garden by Mary Hickey
Biblical Blocks by Rosemary Makhan
Blockbuster Quilts by Margaret J. Miller
Borders by Design by Paulette Peters
Botanical Wreaths by Laura M. Reinstatler
Calendar Quilts by Joan Hanson
Cathedral Window: A Fresh Look
   by Nancy J. Martin
The Cat's Meow by Janet Kime
A Child's Garden of Quilts
   by Christal Carter
Colourwash Quilts by Deirdre Amsden
Corners in the Cabin by Paulette Peters
Country Medallion Sampler
   by Carol Doak
Country Threads by Connie Tesene and
   Mary Tendall
Decoupage Quilts by Barbara Roberts
Designing Quilts by Suzanne Hammond
The Easy Art of Appliqué
   by Mimi Dietrich & Roxi Eppler
Easy Machine Paper Piecing
   by Carol Doak
Easy Quilts...By Jupiter!®
   by Mary Beth Maison
Easy Reversible Vests by Carol Doak
Fantasy Flowers
   by Doreen Cronkite Burbank
Five- and Seven-Patch Blocks & Quilts for
   the ScrapSaver by Judy Hopkins
Four-Patch Blocks & Quilts for the
   ScrapSaver by Judy Hopkins
Fun with Fat Quarters by Nancy J. Martin
Go Wild with Quilts by Margaret Rolfe
Handmade Quilts by Mimi Dietrich
Happy Endings by Mimi Dietrich
The Heirloom Quilt by Yolande Filson
   and Roberta Przybylski

Holiday Happenings by Christal Carter
In The Beginning by Sharon Evans Yenter
Irma's Sampler by Irma Eskes
Jacket Jazz by Judy Murrah
Jacket Jazz Encore by Judy Murrah
Le Rouvray by Diane de Obaldia,
   with Marie-Christine Flocard and
   Cosabeth Parriaud
Lessons in Machine Piecing
   by Marsha McCloskey
Little Quilts by Alice Berg, Sylvia Johnson,
   and Mary Ellen Von Holt
Lively Little Logs by Donna McConnell
Loving Stitches by Jeana Kimball
Machine Quilting Made Easy
   by Maurine Noble
Make Room for Quilts by Nancy J. Martin
Nifty Ninepatches by Carolann M. Palmer
Nine-Patch Blocks & Quilts for the
   ScrapSaver by Judy Hopkins
Not Just Quilts by Jo Parrott
Oh! Christmas Trees
   compiled by Barbara Weiland
On to Square Two by Marsha McCloskey
Osage County Quilt Factory
   by Virginia Robertson
Our Pieceful Village by Lynn Rice
Painless Borders by Sally Schneider
A Perfect Match by Donna Lynn Thomas
Picture Perfect Patchwork
   by Naomi Norman
Piecemakers® *Country Store*
   by the Piecemakers
Pineapple Passion
   by Nancy Smith and Lynda Milligan
A Pioneer Doll and Her Quilts
   by Mary Hickey
Pioneer Storybook Quilts by Mary Hickey
Prairie People—Cloth Dolls to Make
   and Cherish by Marji Hadley and
   J. Dianne Ridgley
Quick & Easy Quiltmaking by Mary Hickey,
   Nancy J. Martin, Marsha McCloskey
   and Sara Nephew
The Quilted Apple by Laurene Sinema
Quilted for Christmas
   compiled by Ursula Reikes
The Quilters' Companion
   compiled by That Patchwork Place

The Quilting Bee
   by Jackie Wolff and Lori Aluna
Quilting Makes the Quilt by Lee Cleland
Quilts for All Seasons by Christal Carter
Quilts for Baby: Easy as A, B, C
   by Ursula Reikes
Quilts for Kids by Carolann M. Palmer
Quilts from Nature by Joan Colvin
Quilts to Share by Janet Kime
Red Wagon Originals
   by Gerry Kimmel and Linda Brannock
Rotary Riot
   by Judy Hopkins and Nancy J. Martin
Rotary Roundup
   by Judy Hopkins and Nancy J. Martin
Round About Quilts by J. Michelle Watts
Round Robin Quilts
   by Pat Magaret and Donna Slusser
Samplings from the Sea
   by Rosemary Makhan
ScrapMania by Sally Schneider
Seasoned with Quilts by Retta Warehime
Sensational Settings by Joan Hanson
Sewing on the Line
   by Lesly-Claire Greenberg
Shortcuts: A Concise Guide to Rotary
   Cutting by Donna Lynn Thomas
Shortcuts Sampler by Roxanne Carter
Shortcuts to the Top
   by Donna Lynn Thomas
Small Talk by Donna Lynn Thomas
Smoothstitch® *Quilts* by Roxi Eppler
The Stitchin' Post
   by Jean Wells and Lawry Thorn
Stringing Along by Trice Boerens
Strips That Sizzle by Margaret J. Miller
Sunbonnet Sue All Through the Year
   by Sue Linker
Tea Party Time by Nancy J. Martin
Template-Free® *Quiltmaking*
   by Trudie Hughes
Template-Free® *Quilts and Borders*
   by Trudie Hughes
Template-Free® *Stars* by Jo Parrott
Treasures from Yesteryear: Book One
   by Sharon Newman
Two for Your Money by Jo Parrott
Watercolor Quilts
   by Pat Magaret and Donna Slusser
Woven & Quilted by Mary Anne Caplinger

4", 6", 8", & metric Bias Square® • BiRangle™ • Ruby Beholder™ • Pineapple Rule • ScrapMaster • Rotary Rule™ • Rotary Mate™
Shortcuts to America's Best-Loved Quilts (video)

Many titles are available at your local quilt shop. For more information, send $2 for a
color catalog to That Patchwork Place, Inc., PO Box 118, Bothell WA 98041-0118 USA.

☎ Call 1-800-426-3126 for the name and location of the quilt shop nearest you.